21st Century Junior Library

GROWING SOCIAL AWARENESS

Building My Social-Emotional Toolbox

Emily Rose

Published in the United States of America by:

CHERRY LAKE PRESS
2395 South Huron Parkway, Suite 200, Ann Arbor, Michigan 48104
www.cherrylakepress.com

Reading Adviser: Beth Walker Gambro, MS, Ed., Reading Consultant, Yorkville, IL

Photo Credits: © SeventyFour/Shutterstock.com, cover, 1; © Andi Berger/Shutterstock.com, 5; © Irina Wilhauk/Shutterstock.com, 6; © 300 librarians/Shutterstock.com, 7; © Cookie Studio/Shutterstock.com, 8; © Lopolo/Shutterstock.com, 9; © Asier Romero/Shutterstock.com, 10, 11; © FAMILY STOCK/Shutterstock.com, 12; © Ammnezia/Shutterstock.com, 13; © Mark Nazh/Shutterstock.com, 14; © Monkey Business Images/Shutterstock.com, 17; © Luis Molinero/Shutterstock.com, 18; © Nicetoseeya/Shutterstock.com, 19; © Suppachok N/Shutterstock.com, 20; © Patrick Foto/Shutterstock.com, 21 [top]; © Random Illustrator/Shutterstock.com, 21 [bottom]

Copyright © 2023 by Cherry Lake Publishing Group

All rights reserved. No part of this book may be reproduced or utilized in any form or by any means without written permission from the publisher.

Cherry Lake Press is an imprint of Cherry Lake Publishing Group.

Library of Congress Cataloging-in-Publication Data

Names: Rose, Emily (School psychologist), author.
Title: Growing social awareness / by Emily Rose.
Description: Ann Arbor, Michigan : Cherry Lake Publishing, [2022] | Series: Building my social-emotional toolbox | Includes bibliographical references and index. | Audience: Grades 2-3
Identifiers: LCCN 2022005358 | ISBN 9781668909027 (hardcover) | ISBN 9781668910627 (paperback) | ISBN 9781668913802 (pdf) | ISBN 9781668912218 (ebook)
Subjects: LCSH: Social perception in children—Juvenile literature. | Social skills in children—Juvenile literature.
Classification: LCC BF723.S6 R67 2022 | DDC 155.4/182—dc23/eng/20220210
LC record available at https://lccn.loc.gov/2022005358

Cherry Lake Press would like to acknowledge the work of the Partnership for 21st Century Learning, a Network of Battelle for Kids. Please visit http://www.battelleforkids.org/networks/p21 for more information.

Printed in the United States of America
Corporate Graphics

CONTENTS

Different People Feel
Different Things   4

How Our Behavior Impacts
Others—Positively *and* Negatively   10

The Golden Rule   15

Extend Your Learning   20
Glossary   22
Find Out More   23
Index   24
About the Author   24

DIFFERENT PEOPLE FEEL DIFFERENT THINGS

When Michaela learned that recess would be inside today because it was raining, she was excited. Indoor recess meant she could play her favorite board game. But when she looked around the room, she noticed that some kids seemed sad or even mad. She felt confused. "Why isn't everyone else happy, too?" she thought to herself. Michaela asked her friend Khyeem why he was

It's nearly impossible for everyone to feel the same way, even in the same situation!

mad. Khyeem said, "I'm mad because I wanted to play on the jungle gym today. It's my favorite thing to do during recess." Michaela then realized that some things that make *her* happy might not make everyone feel the same way.

Have you ever heard the **phrase**, "Put yourself in someone else's shoes"? This means trying to understand how

Think of a time you put yourself in someone else's shoes. What did you learn?

someone else feels by taking their **perspective**, or their way of looking at things. It is similar to imagining how someone else feels and **responding** in a way that might make them feel understood.

Make a Guess!

How do you think Michaela noticed that other kids felt sad or mad? What do you think the other kids were doing that showed the way they were feeling?

What do you think this person's expression says about their feelings?

Noticing how others feel is not always easy, but there are ways to grow your awareness of the feelings and needs of others. You can look at their facial expressions, such as a smile or a frown, or observe how they are acting. Sometimes people will tell you exactly how they feel, but other times you might have to ask.

Ask Questions!

If you aren't sure how someone else is feeling, take a moment to ask! Even though you might think you know how someone is feeling based on the way they are acting, sometimes you can't know for sure unless the other person tells you.

9

HOW OUR BEHAVIOR IMPACTS OTHERS—POSITIVELY AND NEGATIVELY

We all share this world and the places within it, so it makes sense to think that we all **impact** each other in some way. Depending on the situation, our impact on others might be positive or negative.

When Mason found out that his favorite pencil was missing, he screamed, banged his fists on his

Create!

Make a reminder card to breathe in and out whenever you feel upset like Mason. You might draw a person with an arrow pointing to their nose and another arrow pointing away from their mouth to show breathing in and out. Be creative!

It's important to pay attention to how our actions affect others.

desk, and stomped his feet. The noise Mason was making made it very hard for the rest of his classmates to hear the morning announcements through the loudspeaker. The teacher quietly asked Mason to take three deep breaths and choose another pencil to write with for now. Mason breathed in and out until he started to calm down.

Look!

Pay attention to things happening around you this week. Do you see any actions that might impact others positively or negatively? Look closely at your actions too. You might learn a lot!

By **preventing** his classmates from hearing important information, Mason's actions **affected** others in a negative way. But our **behavior** can affect others in a positive way too.

Aubrey noticed that her friend Deena was sad because her family's dog had passed away. To cheer her up, Aubrey put a nice note in Deena's desk. When Deena opened the note, she felt better knowing that she had a friend who cared about her and her loss.

Remember to always treat others the way you want to be treated.

THE GOLDEN RULE

Practicing social awareness helps you know what someone else needs. Just think about how nice it feels when you are mad or sad and someone *notices* and offers to help you!

Hattie always wants what she wants and often doesn't think about other people. She runs to be first in line for recess, takes the best seat on the bus, and doesn't share the markers during art class. Hattie's friend Layla told her that it wasn't nice to act this way. Hattie said she didn't understand why, because the way she acts makes her happy. So Layla decided one day to show Hattie how she makes other people feel. Layla ran to the front of the line for recess, took the best seat on the bus,

Think!

We all act like Hattie every once in a while. Next time you notice that you are thinking only about yourself and forgetting about others, remember this story. Try to treat others the way you would want to be treated. Many people call this the Golden Rule.

Good teamwork relies on thinking about more than just yourself.

17

Is it easy for you to think of how your behavior might impact others? Why or why not?

and kept the whole box of markers to herself during art class. At the end of the day, Hattie told Layla, "I understand what you mean now. I didn't know how other kids felt when I did those things, but now I do know. I don't like it one bit. I'll pay more attention to other people from now on." This story is an important reminder to always follow the Golden Rule!

EXTEND YOUR LEARNING

Think about your favorite **character** in a book or movie. Now imagine how their behavior might affect others in a positive or negative way. For example, when Nemo from the movie *Finding Nemo* **disobeys** his dad and swims out to sea to touch the boat, how do you think his action made his dad feel? Thinking about how a person's behavior impacts everyone helps us remember to consider other people throughout each day.

GLOSSARY

affected (uh-FEK-tuhd) produced an effect or change on someone or something

behavior (bih-HAY-vyuhr) how someone acts

character (KAIR-ik-tuhr) a person or animal in a book, movie, or TV show

disobeys (diss-uh-BAYS) does not follow orders

impact (IM-pakt) to have an effect on something

perspective (puhr-SPEK-tiv) a person's way of looking at things; point of view

phrase (FRAYZ) a saying or expression

preventing (prih-VENT-ing) stopping something from happening

reminder (rih-MYN-duhr) something that helps you remember something else

responding (rih-SPAHND-ing) answering or acting in response to something

FIND OUT MORE

Books
Murphy, Frank. *Stand Up for Caring.* Ann Arbor, MI: Cherry Lake Publishing, 2019.

Rose, Emily. *Feeling and Showing Empathy.* Ann Arbor, MI: Cherry Lake Publishing, 2022.

Rose, Emily. *Making and Keeping Friends.* Ann Arbor, MI: Cherry Lake Publishing, 2022.

Websites
YouTube—Social Emotional Learning: Social Awareness
https://www.youtube.com/watch?v=reM8uQVqgoM
Watch this video for an example of social awareness.

YouTube—What Does it Mean to "Walk in Someone Else's Shoes"?
https://www.youtube.com/watch?v=0jdQTWy0K4o
Watch this video to learn more about the phrase "Walk in someone else's shoes."

INDEX

behavior
   golden rule and, 15–19
   impacts on others, 10–14, 16–19, 20
body language, 8–9
breathing exercises, 11–12

characters, fictional, 20

differences in preferences, 4–7

emotions and feelings
   asking about, 9
   differences in, 4–7
   empathy, 4–9, 13, 15
   regulation, 11–12
empathy
   aims and methods, 6–9
   examples, 4–6, 13, 15

facial expressions, 8–9
fictional characters, 20

golden rule, 14–16

negative behaviors, 10, 12–13, 15–16, 19–20
nonverbal communication, 8–9

perspective-taking, 6–7
positive behaviors, 10, 13

questions about feelings, 9

teamwork, 17

ABOUT THE AUTHOR

Emily Rose is a school psychologist, yoga teacher, and writer for her mental wellness blog, MissMagnoliaSays.com. She enjoys helping kids and adults understand and manage their emotions and live beautiful lives. Emily lives in Dearborn, Michigan.

Flinn ChemTopic™ Labs Series Preface
Lab Manuals Organized Around Key Content Areas in Chemistry

In conversations with chemistry teachers across the country we have heard a common concern. Teachers are frustrated with their current lab manuals, with experiments that are poorly designed and don't teach core concepts, with procedures that are rigid and inflexible and don't work. Teachers want greater flexibility in their choice of lab activities. As we further listened to experienced master teachers who regularly lead workshops and training seminars, another theme emerged. Master teachers mostly rely on collections of experiments and demonstrations they have put together themselves over the years. Some activities have been passed on like cherished family recipe cards from one teacher to another. Others have been adapted from one format to another to take advantage of new trends in microscale equipment and procedures, technology innovations, and discovery-based learning theory. In all cases the experiments and demonstrations have been fine-tuned based on real classroom experience.

Flinn Scientific has developed a series of lab manuals based on these "cherished recipe cards" of master teachers with proven excellence in both teaching students and training teachers. Created under the direction of an Advisory Board of award-winning chemistry teachers, each lab manual in the Flinn ChemTopic™ Labs series contains 4–6 student-tested experiments that focus on essential concepts and applications in a single content area. Each lab manual also contains 3–5 demonstrations that can be used to illustrate a chemical property, reaction, or relationship and will capture your students' attention. The experiments and demonstrations in the Flinn ChemTopic™ Labs series are enjoyable, highly focused, and will give students a real sense of accomplishment.

Laboratory experiments allow students to experience chemistry by doing chemistry. Experiments have been selected to provide students with a crystal-clear understanding of chemistry concepts and encourage students to think about these concepts critically and analytically. Well-written procedures are guaranteed to work. Reproducible data tables teach students how to organize their data so it is easily analyzed. Comprehensive teacher notes include a master materials list, solution preparation guide, complete sample data, and answers to all questions. Detailed lab hints and teaching tips show you how to conduct the experiment in your lab setting and how to identify student errors and misconceptions before students are led astray.

Chemical demonstrations provide another teaching tool for seeing chemistry in action. Because they are both visual and interactive, demonstrations allow teachers to take students on a journey of observation and understanding. Demonstrations provide additional resources to develop central themes and to magnify the power of observation in the classroom. Demonstrations using discrepant events challenge student misconceptions that must be broken down before new concepts can be learned. Use demonstrations to introduce new ideas, illustrate abstract concepts that cannot be covered in lab experiments, and provide a spark of excitement that will capture student interest and attention.

Safety, flexibility, and choice

Safety always comes first. Depend on Flinn Scientific to give you upfront advice and guidance on all safety and disposal issues. Each activity begins with a description of the hazards involved and the necessary safety precautions to avoid exposure to these hazards. Additional safety, handling, and disposal information is also contained in the teacher notes.

The selection of experiments and demonstrations in each Flinn ChemTopic™ Labs manual gives you the flexibility to choose activities that match the concepts your students need to learn. No single teacher will do all of the experiments and demonstrations with a single class. Some experiments and demonstrations may be more helpful with a beginning-level class, while others may be more suitable with an honors class. All of the experiments and demonstrations have been keyed to national content standards in science education.

Chemistry is an experimental science!

Whether they are practicing key measurement skills or searching for trends in the chemical properties of substances, all students will benefit from the opportunity to discover chemistry by doing chemistry. No matter what chemistry textbook you use in the classroom, Flinn ChemTopic™ Labs will help you give your students the necessary knowledge, skills, attitudes, and values to be successful in chemistry.

About the Curriculum Advisory Board

Flinn Scientific is honored to work with an outstanding group of dedicated chemistry teachers. The members of the Flinn ChemTopic Labs Advisory Board have generously contributed their proven experiments, demonstrations, and teaching tips to create these topic lab manuals. The wisdom, experience, creativity, and insight reflected in their lab activities guarantee that students who perform them will be more successful in learning chemistry. On behalf of all chemistry teachers, we thank the Advisory Board members for their service to the teaching profession and their dedication to the field of chemistry education.

Bob Becker teaches chemistry and AP chemistry at Kirkwood High School in Kirkwood, MO. Bob received his B.A. from Yale University and M.Ed. from Washington University and has 15 years of teaching experience. A well-known demonstrator, Bob has conducted more than 100 demonstration workshops across the U.S. and Canada and is currently a Team Leader for the Flinn Foundation Summer Workshop Program. His creative and unusual demonstrations have been published in the *Journal of Chemical Education,* the *Science Teacher,* and *Chem13 News.* Bob is the author of two books of chemical demonstrations, *Twenty Demonstrations Guaranteed to Knock Your Socks Off, Volumes I and II,* published by Flinn Scientific. Bob has been awarded the James Bryant Conant Award in High School Teaching from the American Chemical Society, the Regional Catalyst Award from the Chemical Manufacturers Association, and the Tandy Technology Scholar Award.

Kathleen J. Dombrink teaches chemistry and advanced-credit college chemistry at McCluer North High School in Florissant, MO. Kathleen received her B.A. in Chemistry from Holy Names College and M.S. in Chemistry from St. Louis University and has more than 30 years of teaching experience. Recognized for her strong support of professional development, Kathleen has been selected to participate in the Fulbright Memorial Fund Teacher Program in Japan and NEWMAST and Dow/NSTA Workshops. She served as co-editor of the inaugural issues of *Chem Matters* and was a Woodrow Wilson National Fellowship Foundation Chemistry Team Member for more than 10 years. Kathleen is currently a Team Leader for the Flinn Foundation Summer Workshop Program. Kathleen has received the Presidential Award, the Midwest Regional Teaching Award from the American Chemical Society, the Tandy Technology Scholar Award, and a Regional Catalyst Award from the Chemical Manufacturers Association.

Robert Lewis teaches chemistry and AP chemistry at Downers Grove North High School in Downers Grove, IL. Robert received his B.A. from North Central College and M.A. from University of the South and has more than 25 years of teaching experience. He was a founding member of Weird Science, a group of chemistry teachers that has traveled throughout the country to stimulate teacher interest and enthusiasm for using demonstrations to teach science. Robert was a Chemistry Team Leader for the Woodrow Wilson National Fellowship Foundation and is currently a Team Leader for the Flinn Foundation Summer Workshop Program. Robert has received the Presidential Award, the James Bryant Conant Award in High School Teaching from the American Chemical Society, the Tandy Technology Scholar Award, a Regional Catalyst Award from the Chemical Manufacturers Association, and a Golden Apple Award from the State of Illinois.

John G. Little teaches chemistry and AP chemistry at St. Mary's High School in Stockton, CA. John received his B.S. and M.S. in Chemistry from University of the Pacific and has more than 35 years of teaching experience. Highly respected for his well-designed labs, John is the author of two lab manuals, *Chemistry Microscale Laboratory Manual* (DC Heath), and *Microscale Experiments for General Chemistry* (with Kenneth Williamson, Houghton Mifflin). He is also a contributing author to *Science Explorer* (Prentice Hall) and *World of Chemistry* (McDougal Littell). John served as a Chemistry Team Leader for the Woodrow Wilson National Fellowship Foundation from 1988 to 1997 and is currently a Team Leader for the Flinn Foundation Summer Workshop Program. He has been recognized for his dedicated teaching with the Tandy Technology Scholar Award and the Regional Catalyst Award from the Chemical Manufacturers Association.

Lee Marek teaches chemistry and AP chemistry at Naperville North High School in Naperville, IL. Lee received his B.S. in Chemical Engineering from the University of Illinois and M.S. degrees in both Physics and Chemistry from Roosevelt University. He has more than 30 years of teaching experience and is currently a Team Leader for the Flinn Foundation Summer Workshop Program. His students have won national recognition in the International Chemistry Olympiad, the Westinghouse Science Talent Search, and the Internet Science and Technology Fair. Lee was a founding member of ChemWest, a regional chemistry teachers alliance, and led this group for 14 years. Together with two other ChemWest members, Lee also founded Weird Science and has presented 500 demonstration and teaching workshops for more than 300,000 students and teachers across the country. Lee has performed science demonstrations on the *David Letterman Show* 20 times. Lee has received the Presidential Award, the James Bryant Conant Award in High School Teaching from the American Chemical Society, the National Catalyst Award from the Chemical Manufacturers Association, and the Tandy Technology Scholar Award.

John Mauch teaches chemistry and AP chemistry at Braintree High School in Braintree, MA. John received his B.A. in Chemistry from Whitworth College and M.A. in Curriculum and Education from Washington State University and has 25 years of teaching experience. John is an expert in "writing to learn" in the chemistry curriculum and in microscale chemistry. He is the author of two lab manuals, *Chemistry in Microscale, Volumes I and II* (Kendall/Hunt). He is also a dynamic and prolific demonstrator and workshop leader. John has presented the Flinn Scientific Chem Demo Extravaganza show at NSTA conventions for seven years and has conducted more than 100 workshops across the country. John was a Chemistry Team Member for the Woodrow Wilson National Fellowship Foundation program for four years and is currently a Team Leader for the Flinn Foundation Summer Workshop Program.

Dave Tanis is Associate Professor of Chemistry at Grand Valley State University in Allendale, MI. Dave received his B.S. in Physics and Mathematics from Calvin College and M.S. in Chemistry from Case Western Reserve University. He taught high school chemistry for 25 years before joining the staff at Grand Valley State University to direct a coalition for improving pre-college math and science education. Dave later joined the faculty at Grand Valley State University and currently teaches courses for pre-service teachers. The author of two laboratory manuals, Dave acknowledges the influence of early encounters with Hubert Alyea, Marge Gardner, Henry Heikkinen, and Bassam Shakhashiri in stimulating his long-standing interest in chemical demonstrations and experiments. Continuing this tradition of mentorship, Dave has led more than 40 one-week institutes for chemistry teachers and served as a Team Member for the Woodrow Wilson National Fellowship Foundation for 13 years. He is currently a Board Member for the Flinn Foundation Summer Workshop Program. Dave received the College Science Teacher of the Year Award from the Michigan Science Teachers Association.

Table of Contents

	Page
Flinn ChemTopic™ Labs Series Preface	i
About the Curriculum Advisory Board	ii
Acids and Bases Preface	iii
Format and Features	iv–v
Experiment Summaries and Concepts	vi–vii

Experiments

Properties of Acids and Bases	1
Natural Indicators	15
Measuring Acid Strength	31
Classic Titration	41
Microscale Titration	55
Buffers Keep the Balance	67

Demonstrations

Indicator Sponge	79
The Rainbow Tube	81
Upset Tummy? MOM to the Rescue!	83
Strong vs. Weak Acids	85
Buffer Balancing Acts	87

Supplementary Information

Safety and Disposal Guidelines	90
National Science Education Standards	92
Master Materials Guide	94

Flinn Scientific
ChemTopic™ Labs

Acids and Bases

Senior Editor

Irene Cesa
Flinn Scientific, Inc.
Batavia, IL

Curriculum Advisory Board

Bob Becker
Kirkwood High School
Kirkwood, MO

Kathleen J. Dombrink
McCluer North High School
Florissant, MO

Robert Lewis
Downers Grove North High School
Downers Grove, IL

John G. Little
St. Mary's High School
Stockton, CA

Lee Marek
Naperville North High School
Naperville, IL

John Mauch
Braintree High School
Braintree, MA

Dave Tanis
Grand Valley State University
Allendale, MI

FLINN SCIENTIFIC INC.
"Your Safer Source for Science Supplies"
P.O. Box 219 • Batavia, IL 60510
1-800-452-1261 • www.flinnsci.com

ISBN 1-877991-81-3

Copyright © 2002 Flinn Scientific, Inc.

All rights reserved. No part of this book may be reproduced or transmitted in any form or by any means, electronic or mechanical, including, but not limited to photocopy, recording, or any information storage and retrieval system, without permission in writing from Flinn Scientific, Inc.
No part of this book may be included on any web site.

Reproduction permission is granted only to the science teacher who has purchased this volume of Flinn ChemTopic™ Labs, Acids and Bases, Catalog No. AP6260 from Flinn Scientific, Inc.
Science teachers may make copies of the reproducible student pages for use only by their students.

Printed in the United States of America.

Preface
Acids and Bases

Vinegar, aspirin, Vitamin C, baking soda, ammonia—many familiar substances that we use every day are acids or bases. Acids and bases are also among the most common and useful reagents in the lab. Indeed, their uses span a wide range of applications, from dissolving metals to catalyzing reactions. The purpose of *Acids and Bases,* Volume 13 in the Flinn ChemTopic™ Labs series, is to bring together in one place a representative selection of acid–base lab activities for the high school chemistry classroom. Six experiments and five demonstrations allow teachers and students to fully explore the properties, principles, and applications of acid–base chemistry.

Identify and classify

Acids and bases are classified based on their physical and chemical properties. In "Properties of Acids and Bases," students test substances on a microscale level using conductivity, indicators, and chemical reactions and use the results to identify and classify acids and bases. "Natural Indicators" is an inquiry-based experiment that allows students to explore the origin of acid–base indicators in nature. Students extract natural indicators from flowers and fruits of their choice and examine their color changes with known acids and bases. The pH scale literally comes to life in living color as students further classify a variety of unknown solutions. Two demonstrations, "Indicator Sponge" and "The Rainbow Tube," round out the selection of lab activities that may be used to introduce the topic of acids and bases and illustrate their properties.

Strong versus weak acids

Acids vary greatly in their strength—their ability to produce ions when dissolved in water. Why do some acids have lower pH values than others, even though their concentrations are the same? Use the "Strong vs. Weak Acids" demonstration to compare the activity and distinguish between strong and weak acids. In "Measuring Acid Strength," students use a simple but elegant procedure to tackle a difficult concept, the nature and magnitude of the equilibrium constant (K_a) for ionization of a weak acid.

Measure and analyze

One of the most common questions chemists have to answer is how much of something is present in a sample or product. If the product contains an acid or base, this question is usually answered by titration. In "Classic Titration," students measure a titration curve for neutralization of a strong acid with a strong base and then analyze the concentration of an unknown strong acid solution. Instructions have been provided for both technology-based and manual data collection and analysis. The principles and applications of titration reactions have been adapted to the microscale level in "Microscale Titration," in which students analyze the percent acetic acid in vinegar.

Biological and consumer applications

Acid–base balance is a true vital sign—in living cells, lakes and streams, even consumer products. In "Buffers Keep the Balance," students investigate the preparation and properties of model solutions that mimic natural biological buffers. Students learn what buffers are made of, how they work, and why different buffers are effective in different pH ranges. Two demonstrations also illustrate the principles and applications of acid–base chemistry in consumer products. "Upset Tummy? MOM to the Rescue!" reveals the role of neutralization reactions in antacid chemistry, while "Buffer Balancing Acts" highlights the physiological role of buffers within cells and in consumer products.

Safety, flexibility and choice

Depend on Flinn Scientific to give you the information and resources to help your students learn to love chemistry. The selection of experiments and demonstrations in *Acids and Bases*—combined with complete sample data and teacher notes—lets every teacher be a leader in the classroom. Your students will appreciate not only the range of activities but also the way in which they bring abstract principles to life. Beginning-level students will thrive as they learn to construct their own working definitions of important concepts in "Properties of Acids and Bases." The intersection of technology- and microscale-based approaches in "Classic Titration" and "Microscale Titration" accommodates students with different interests and learning styles. All students will enjoy the surprise and satisfaction of working with natural products in "Natural Indicators." Finally, because each experiment in *Acids and Bases* has been thoroughly tested and retested, your students are assured of success. Use the experiment summaries and concepts on the following pages to locate the concepts you want to teach and to choose experiments and demonstrations that will help you meet your goals.

Format and Features

Flinn ChemTopic™ Labs

All experiments and demonstrations in Flinn ChemTopic™ Labs are printed in a $10\frac{7}{8}'' \times 11''$ format with a wide 2" margin on the inside of each page. This reduces the printed area of each page to a standard $8\frac{1}{2}'' \times 11''$ format suitable for copying.

The wide margin assures you the entire printed area can be easily reproduced without hurting the binding. The margin also provides a convenient place for teachers to add their own notes.

Concepts — Use these bulleted lists along with state and local standards, lesson plans, and your textbook to identify activities that will allow you to accomplish specific learning goals and objectives.

Background — A balanced source of information for students to understand why they are doing an experiment, what they are doing, and the types of questions the activity is designed to answer. This section is not meant to be exhaustive or to replace the students' textbook, but rather to identify the core concepts that should be covered before starting the lab.

Experiment Overview — Clearly defines the purpose of each experiment and how students will achieve this goal. Performing an experiment without a purpose is like getting travel directions without knowing your destination. It doesn't work, especially if you run into a roadblock and need to take a detour!

Pre-Lab Questions — Making sure that students are prepared for lab is the single most important element of lab safety. Pre-lab questions introduce new ideas or concepts, review key calculations, and reinforce safety recommendations. The pre-lab questions may be assigned as homework in preparation for lab or they may be used as the basis of a cooperative class activity before lab.

Materials — Lists chemical names, formulas, and amounts for all reagents—along with specific glassware and equipment—needed to perform the experiment as written. The material dispensing area is a main source of student delay, congestion, and accidents. Three dispensing stations per room are optimum for a class of 24 students working in pairs. To safely substitute different items for any of the recommended materials, refer to the *Lab Hints* section in each experiment or demonstration.

Safety Precautions — Instruct and warn students of the hazards associated with the materials or procedure and give specific recommendations and precautions to protect students from these hazards. Please review this section with students before beginning each experiment.

Procedure — This section contains a stepwise, easy-to-follow procedure, where each step generally refers to one action item. Contains reminders about safety and recording data where appropriate. For inquiry-based experiments the procedure may restate the experiment objective and give general guidelines for accomplishing this goal.

Data Tables — Data tables are included for each experiment and are referred to in the procedure. These are provided for convenience and to teach students the importance of keeping their data organized in order to analyze it. To encourage more student involvement, many teachers prefer to have students prepare their own data tables. This is an excellent pre-lab preparation activity—it ensures that students have read the procedure and are prepared for lab.

Post-Lab Questions or Data Analysis — This section takes students step-by-step through what they did, what they observed, and what it means. Meaningful questions encourage analysis and promote critical thinking skills. Where students need to perform calculations or graph data to analyze the results, these steps are also laid out sequentially and in order.

Format and Features
Teacher's Notes

Master Materials List

Lists the chemicals, glassware, and equipment needed to perform the experiment. All amounts have been calculated for a class of 30 students working in pairs. For smaller or larger class sizes or different working group sizes, please adjust the amounts proportionately.

Preparation of Solutions

Calculations and procedures are given for preparing all solutions, based on a class size of 30 students working in pairs. With the exception of particularly hazardous materials, the solution amounts generally include 10% extra to account for spillage and waste. Solution volumes may be rounded to convenient glassware sizes (100 mL, 250 mL, 500 mL, etc.)

Safety Precautions

Repeats the safety precautions given to the students and includes more detailed information relating to safety and handling of chemicals and glassware. Refers to Material Safety Data Sheets that should be available for all chemicals used in the laboratory.

Disposal

Refers to the current *Flinn Scientific Catalog/Reference Manual* for general guidelines and specific procedures governing the disposal of laboratory waste. Because we recommend that teachers review local regulations before beginning any disposal procedure, the information given in this section is for general reference purposes only. However, if a disposal step is included as part of the experimental procedure itself, then the specific solutions needed for disposal are described in this section.

Lab Hints

This section reveals common sources of student errors and misconceptions and where students are likely to need help. Identifies the recommended length of time needed to perform each experiment, suggests alternative chemicals and equipment that may be used, and reminds teachers about new techniques (filtration, pipeting, etc.) that should be reviewed prior to lab.

Teaching Tips

This section puts the experiment in perspective so that teachers can judge in more detail how and where a particular experiment will fit into their curriculum. Identifies the working assumptions about what students need to know in order to perform the experiment and answer the questions. Highlights historical background and applications-oriented information that may be of interest to students.

Sample Data

Complete, actual sample data obtained by performing the experiment exactly as written is included for each experiment. Student data will vary.

Answers to All Questions

Representative or typical answers to all questions. Includes sample calculations and graphs for all data analysis questions. Information of special interest to teachers only in this section is identified by the heading "Note to the teacher." Student answers will vary.

Look for these icons in the *Experiment Summaries and Concepts* section and in the *Teacher's Notes* of individual experiments to identify inquiry-, microscale-, and technology-based experiments, respectively.

Experiment Summaries and Concepts

Experiment

Properties of Acids and Bases—Identification and Classification

Acids and bases are useful reagents in the laboratory and play an important role in biology and nature. What properties of substances can be used to distinguish acids and bases? The purpose of this microscale experiment is to explore the properties of aqueous solutions and classify them as acidic, basic, or neutral. The results of indicator, reactivity, and conductivity tests are used to develop working definitions of acids and bases and to analyze the pH scale for identifying acids and bases.

Natural Indicators—Acids, Bases, and the pH Scale

Roses are red, violets are blue—or are they? Red roses, as well as many other flowers and fruits, contain natural indicators that are sensitive to acids and bases. In this inquiry-based activity, students extract natural indicators from flowers and fruits and then design a procedure to investigate their color changes as a function of pH. The results are used to analyze the pH values of unknown solutions.

Measuring Acid Strength—K_a Values of Weak Acids

Acids vary greatly in their strength—their ability to produce ions when dissolved in water. What factors determine the strength of an acid? The purpose of this experiment is to measure the equilibrium constant for ionization of an unknown weak acid. Solutions containing equal molar amounts of a weak acid and its conjugate base are prepared by half-neutralization of the acid. Their pH values are measured and used to calculate the K_a value of the acid and determine its identity.

Classic Titration—pH Curves and an Unknown

One of the most common questions chemists have to answer is how much of something is present in a sample or product. If the product contains an acid or base, this question is usually answered by titration. The purpose of this technology-based activity is to analyze the shape of the titration curve for neutralization of hydrochloric acid with sodium hydroxide and to determine the concentration of an unknown hydrochloric acid solution.

Microscale Titration—Percent Acetic Acid in Vinegar

Vinegar, aspirin, antacids—many common substances that we use every day are acids or bases. The composition or purity of these products is something we normally take for granted. In this experiment, students analyze the percent acetic acid in vinegar by microscale titration. Students prepare a standard sodium hydroxide solution of known molarity and then use this solution to titrate vinegar and determine the percent of acetic acid.

Buffers Keep the Balance—Biological Buffers

A buffer protects against changes in pH when acids and bases are added to it. Every living cell contains natural buffer systems that maintain the constant pH needed for proper cell function. Consumer products are often buffered to safeguard their activity. The purpose of this experiment is to explore the properties of model carbonate and phosphate buffers that mimic the biological buffers present in blood and cells, respectively.

Concepts

- Acids and bases
- pH Scale
- Indicators
- Conductivity

- Indicators
- Extraction
- pH Scale

- Weak acid
- Conjugate base
- Equilibrium constant
- Neutralization reaction

- Titration
- Neutralization
- Equivalence point
- Titration curve

- Microscale titration
- Neutralization
- Equivalence point
- Molarity

- pH
- Buffer
- Weak acid
- Conjugate base

Experiment Summaries and Concepts

Demonstration

Indicator Sponge—A Discrepant Event Demonstration

Place a red sponge in a red solution, and it comes out blue! This discrepant event demonstration will capture your students' attention and stimulate a lively discussion of possible explanations. Use the indicator sponge to introduce the properties of acid–base indicators and how substances are classified as acids or bases.

The Rainbow Tube Chemical Demonstration

Saturated sodium carbonate solution is added to a test tube containing a dilute solution of hydrochloric acid and universal indicator. A rainbow column of colors develops in the tube as the dense sodium carbonate solution sinks to the bottom and carbonate ions diffuse upward and neutralize the hydrochloric acid.

Upset Tummy? MOM to the Rescue—Colorful Antacid Demonstration

Mix milk of magnesia with universal indicator and add hydrochloric acid solution. Observe a dramatic spectrum of color changes as the antacid dissolves in and neutralizes the simulated stomach acid. This is a great demonstration to illustrate principles and consumer applications of acid–base chemistry.

Strong vs. Weak Acids Chemical Demonstration

Not all acids are created equal! This demonstration compares the "frothing and foaming" activity of two acids with calcium carbonate and examines their behavior in the presence of their conjugate bases to distinguish strong versus weak acids. The pH scale, hydrogen ion concentrations, rates of reaction, and equilibrium all come together in this engaging demonstration.

Buffer Balancing Acts Chemical Demonstration

Buffers provide an essential acid–base balancing act—in consumer products, foods, lakes and streams, and even living cells. What are buffers made of and how do they work? The ability of phosphate buffer and Alka-Seltzer solutions to resist pH changes highlights the physiological role of buffers within cells and in consumer products.

Concepts

- Acids and bases
- Indicators

- Acids and bases
- Indicators
- pH Scale
- Neutralization

- Acids and bases
- Solubility
- Neutralization
- Antacids

- Strong acid
- Weak acid
- Conjugate base
- pH

- pH
- Buffer
- Weak acid
- Conjugate base

Page 1 – **Properties of Acids and Bases**

Teacher Notes

Properties of Acids and Bases
Identification and Classification

Introduction

Acids and bases are useful reagents in the chemistry laboratory and play an important role in biology and nature. What are acids and bases? What properties can be used to distinguish acids and bases? Let's explore the properties of acids and bases and identify the characteristic features that will allow us to classify substances as acids and bases.

Concepts

- Acids and bases
- Active metals
- pH Scale
- Indicators
- Conductivity
- Neutralization

Background

The word acid is derived from the Latin verb *acere* which means "to (be) sour." The origin of the word acid reveals a characteristic physical property of acids—they taste sour. Lemons, oranges, and grapefruits are called citrus fruits because they contain citric acid, an acidic compound which gives them their sour taste. Although taste is an interesting property of the foods we eat, it is NOT a property that we will use in the chemical laboratory to classify compounds as acids or bases. The following properties are typically used to classify compounds as acids or bases.

Conductivity. Some acids and bases ionize completely into ions when dissolved in water. Solutions that contain large numbers of dissolved ions conduct an electric current and are called electrolytes. Other weaker acids and bases may ionize only partially when dissolved in water and may conduct electricity only weakly—they are called weak electrolytes. Substances that do not produce dissolved ions will not conduct electricity and are called nonelectrolytes.

Effect on Indicators. Indicators are organic dyes that change color in acidic or basic solutions. One of the oldest known acid–base indicators is litmus, a natural dye obtained from lichens. Its use was described as early as the sixteenth century. Litmus paper, prepared by soaking paper in a solution of the dye, is often used as a general test for acids and bases. Phenolphthalein is another indicator that shows a color change as solutions change from acidic to basic. Although these indicators are useful for broadly classifying substances as acids or bases, they are not able to distinguish among different levels of acidity or basicity. By using combinations of different indicators, however, it is possible to obtain a spectrum of color changes over a wide range of acidity levels. Universal indicator and pH paper are two products that use combinations of indicators to rank substances from most acidic to least acidic, or most basic to least basic.

The pH Scale. The pH scale is a numerical scale that is used to describe the relative acidity or basicity of a solution and is related to the concentration of H_3O^+ ions. The abbreviation pH stands for "power of hydrogen"—a difference of one unit on the pH scale corresponds to a power of ten difference in the concentration of H_3O^+ ions. Pure water contains extremely

The notation H_3O^+ is used throughout this book to represent hydrogen ions in aqueous solution. Some texts use the notation $H^+(aq)$ instead. Neither symbol completely represents the exact nature of hydrated ions in solution.

Properties of Acids and Bases

Properties of Acids and Bases – *Page 2*

small, but equal, concentrations of H_3O^+ and OH^- ions due to self-ionization *(Equation 1)*. Acids and bases are substances that alter the concentrations of H_3O^+ and OH^- ions in solution.

$$H_2O(l) + H_2O(l) \rightarrow H_3O^+(aq) + OH^-(aq) \qquad \textit{Equation 1}$$

Reaction with Metals. Acids react with so-called *active metals*—reactive metals such as magnesium and zinc—to produce hydrogen gas and solutions of metal ions. The reaction of different metals with acids is a well-known test used to rank metals from most active to least active. Reaction of a single active metal with a variety of different solutions is one of the best methods to identify acids and to compare their relative acidity.

Neutralization reactions. Acids and bases react with each other to give *neutral* products—solutions that are neither acidic nor basic. The products of neutralization of an acid and a base are an ionic compound (generally referred to as a salt) and water. The amount of acid that will react with a specific amount of base is governed by stoichiometry. Neutralization reactions are frequently used in the laboratory to determine how much of an acidic or basic compound is present in a substance.

Experiment Overview

The purpose of this experiment is to explore the properties of aqueous solutions and to classify them as acidic, basic, or neutral. The results will be used to develop working definitions and to analyze the pH scale for identifying acids and bases.

Pre-Lab Questions

Acid wit, acid rain, and an acid test—these familiar expressions suggest some interesting properties and uses of acids.

1. The phrase *acid wit* is defined in the dictionary as humor that is sharp, biting, or sour in nature. In the laboratory, acids present a hazard because they are corrosive. What is meant by the term corrosive? How does this relate to acid wit?

2. *Acid rain* is recognized as a growing danger to the environment. Briefly describe two problems associated with acid rain.

3. *(Optional)* The phrase *acid test* has entered the popular vocabulary to describe a severe but conclusive test of whether something is authentic. What is the origin of the term acid test?

Materials

Acetic acid solution, CH_3COOH, 0.1 M, 6 mL
Ammonia solution, NH_3, 0.1 M, 4 mL
Hydrochloric acid solution, HCl, 0.1 M, 6 mL
Magnesium ribbon or turnings, Mg, 5 pieces
Phenolphthalein solution, 0.5% in alcohol, 2 mL
Sodium hydroxide solution, NaOH, 0.1 M, 8 mL
Universal indicator, 1 mL
Wash bottle and distilled or deionized water

Conductivity tester
Forceps
Litmus paper, neutral, 5 pieces
pH test strips, wide range
Pipets, Beral-type, 5
Reaction plate, 24-well
Stirring rod
White paper (for background)

Teacher Notes

Toothpicks may also be used as mini-stirring rods to mix solutions in well plates.

Page 3 – **Properties of Acids and Bases**

Teacher Notes

Safety Precautions

All of the acids and bases used in this lab are corrosive to eyes, skin, and other body tissues. They are toxic by ingestion. Avoid contact of all chemicals with eyes and skin. Notify your teacher and clean up all spills immediately with large amounts of water. Magnesium metal is a flammable solid and burns with an intense flame. Keep away from flames. Phenolphthalein is an alcohol-based solution and is flammable. It is moderately toxic by ingestion. Keep away from flames and other ignition sources. Wear chemical splash goggles and chemical-resistant gloves and apron. Wash hands thoroughly with soap and water before leaving the laboratory.

Procedure

Part A. Classifying Acids and Bases

1. Obtain a 24-well reaction plate and place it on a piece of white paper as shown below. Note that each well is identified by a unique combination of a letter and number, where the letter refers to the horizontal row and the number to the vertical column.

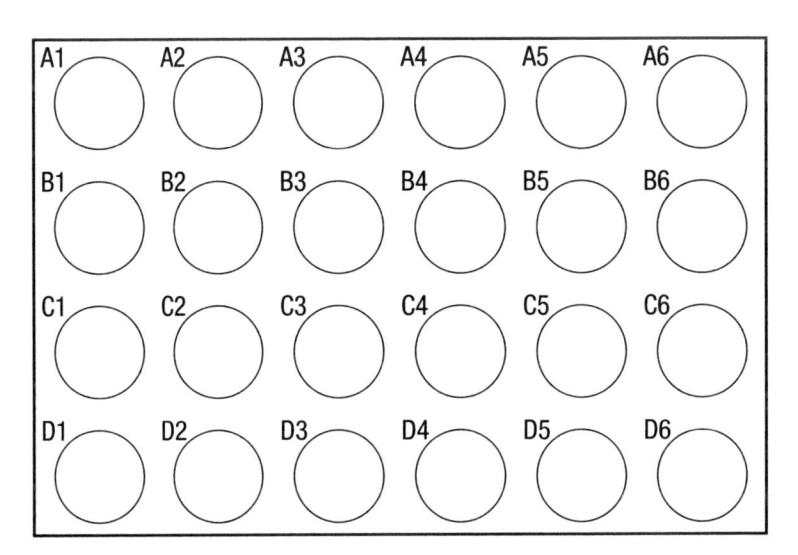

2. Label five pipets 1–5 and fill them with solution, as shown below.

Label	1	2	3	4	5
Solution	Hydrochloric Acid	Acetic Acid	Distilled Water	Ammonia	Sodium Hydroxide

3. Fill wells A1–A5 in Row A about two-thirds full with the corresponding solutions 1–5. *Note:* The wells in a 24-well reaction plate have a 3-mL capacity. Add about 2 mL (40 drops) of solution to each well.

The exact number of drops used in Part A is not crucial. In Part B, however, the number of drops must be precisely added in order to obtain meaningful results.

4. Test each solution in Row A (wells A1–A5) using a conductivity tester. Describe each solution as a strong conductor, weak conductor, or non-conductor and record any additional observations in Data Table A. Rinse the conductivity tester with distilled water and wipe clean between each test.

5. Test each solution in Row A (wells A1–A5) using a piece of neutral litmus paper. Record the color of the paper in Data Table A. *Note:* Dip a stirring rod into the solution, then

Properties of Acids and Bases

Properties of Acids and Bases – Page 4

touch the stirring rod to the test paper. When used in this way, one test paper may be used for more than one solution. Be sure to wipe the stirring rod clean before testing each new solution.

6. Add 1 drop of phenolphthalein solution to each well A1–A5. Record the color of each solution in Data Table A.

7. Add 20 drops of solutions 1–5 to the corresponding wells B1–B5 in Row B.

8. Test each solution in Row B (wells B1–B5) using a pH test strip. Use the color chart on the pH paper container to assign a numerical pH value to each solution. Record the pH value for each solution in Data Table A.

9. Add 1 drop of universal indicator to each well B1–B5. Record the color of each solution in Data Table A.

10. Add 20 drops of solutions 1–5 to the corresponding wells C1–C5 in Row C.

11. Add one small piece of magnesium metal to each solution in wells C1–C5. Observe any apparent reaction that takes place and compare the speed of reaction, if any, in each well. Record all observations in Data Table A.

Part B. Neutralization Reactions of Acids and Bases

12. Carefully add 20 drops of hydrochloric acid (solution 1), followed by 1 drop of phenolphthalein, to each well D1 and D2.

13. Carefully add sodium hydroxide (solution 5) *one drop at a time* to the solution in well D1 until a stable color change occurs. Stir the solution in between drops. Record the number of drops of sodium hydroxide added (Trial 1) in Data Table B.

14. Add 10 drops of distilled water to the solution in well D2. Repeat step 13 to test the solution in well D2. Record the number of drops of sodium hydroxide added (Trial 2) in Data Table B.

15. Carefully add 20 drops of acetic acid (solution 2), followed by 1 drop of phenolphthalein, to each well D5 and D6.

16. Carefully add sodium hydroxide (solution 5) *one drop at a time* to the solution in well D5 until a color change occurs. Record the number of drops of sodium hydroxide added (Trial 1) in Data Table B.

17. Add 10 drops of distilled water to the solution in well D6. Repeat step 16 to test the solution in well D6. Record the number of drops of sodium hydroxide added (Trial 2) in Data Table B.

Disposal

18. Using forceps, remove any pieces of unreacted metal from wells C1–C5. Dispose of these metal pieces as instructed by your teacher. Rinse the contents of the reaction plate down the drain with plenty of excess water.

Teacher Notes

See the Lab Hints section for a description of an optional "burning match" test to identify hydrogen in the reaction of magnesium with acids.

Teacher Notes

Name: _____

Class/Lab Period: _____

Properties of Acids and Bases

Data Table A. *Classifying Acids and Bases*

Test Property	Solution				
	1	2	3	4	5
	Hydrochloric Acid	Acetic Acid	Distilled Water	Ammonia	Sodium Hydroxide
Conductivity					
Litmus Paper					
Phenolphthalein					
pH Test Paper					
Universal Indicator					
Reaction with Magnesium					

Data Table B. *Neutralization Reactions of Acids and Bases*

	Hydrochloric Acid	Acetic Acid
Number of Drops of Sodium Hydroxide Added (Trial 1)		
Number of Drops of Sodium Hydroxide Added (Trial 2)		

In Part B, it is important that the size and number of drops of each reagent be precisely added.

Properties of Acids and Bases

Properties of Acids and Bases – Page 6

Post-Lab Questions *(Use a separate sheet of paper to answer the following questions.)*

1. Use the results of the conductivity test to identify each solution in Part A as a strong electrolyte, weak electrolyte, or nonelectrolyte.

2. Which solutions in Part A reacted with magnesium metal? Write a balanced chemical equation for the reaction of each acid in Part A with magnesium.

3. *Strong acids* ionize completely in water to form ions and are thus strong electrolytes. In contrast, *weak acids* do not readily ionize in water—in fact, less than 1% of the molecules are probably ionized at any given time. Weak acids are therefore weak electrolytes. Classify each acid as either a strong or weak acid. Which reacted faster with magnesium metal, the strong acid or the weak acid?

4. Write chemical equations for ionization of the strong and weak acids in water. Identify the common ion that is produced in acidic solutions.

5. How can litmus paper and phenolphthalein be used to tell whether a solution is an acid or a base? Be specific.

6. Use the combined results of the conductivity and indicator tests to identify the basic solutions in Part A. Classify each as a *strong* versus *weak* base.

7. Write chemical equations for the ion-forming reactions of the strong and weak bases in water. Identify the common ion that is produced in basic solutions.

8. Compare the pH data for the solutions which you labeled as acids and bases. What pH values can be assigned to acids and bases, respectively?

9. Compare the pH values of strong versus weak acid and strong versus weak base solutions. How does pH vary with the "strength" of an acid or base, respectively?

10. Explain the color change observed for the indicator in the neutralization reaction of hydrochloric acid in Part B. What is the pH range of the final solution?

11. (a) Write separate, balanced equations for the neutralization reactions of hydrochloric acid and acetic acid with sodium hydroxide.

    (b) Use the stoichiometry of the balanced chemical equations to explain the number of drops of sodium hydroxide required for complete neutralization of the acids.

    (c) Did the strong and weak acids require equal number of drops of sodium hydroxide? Explain.

    (d) Did adding water to the acid solutions change the number of drops of sodium hydroxide required for neutralization? Explain.

12. Complete the following table to summarize the properties of acids and bases.

Property	Acids	Bases
Conductivity		
Litmus		
Phenolphthalein		
Reaction with metals		
pH		

Teacher Notes

Flinn ChemTopic™ Labs — Acids and Bases

Teacher Notes

Teacher's Notes
Properties of Acids and Bases

Master Materials List *(for a class of 30 students working in pairs)*

Acetic acid solution, CH_3COOH, 0.1 M, 100 mL	Conductivity testers,* 5
Ammonia solution, NH_3, 0.1 M, 75 mL	Forceps, 15
Hydrochloric acid solution, HCl, 0.1 M, 100 mL	Litmus paper, neutral, 1 vial
Magnesium ribbon or turnings, 6 g	pH test strips (wide range), pH 1–12
Phenolphthalein solution, 0.5% in alcohol, 50 mL	Pipets, Beral-type, 75
Sodium hydroxide solution, NaOH, 0.1 M, 150 mL	Reaction plates, 24-well, 15
Universal indicator solution, 25 mL	Stirring rods, 15
Wash bottles and distilled or deionized water, 15	White paper (for background)

*Several groups may share a conductivity tester. See the *Lab Hints* section for a description of a small-scale conductivity tester (Flinn Catalog No. AP1493).

Preparation of Solutions *(for a class of 30 students working in pairs)*

Acetic Acid, 0.1 M: Add about 50 mL of distilled or deionized water to a flask. Carefully add 0.57 mL of glacial (17.4 M) acetic acid. Stir to mix, then dilute to 100 mL with distilled water.

Ammonia, 0.1 M: Add about 50 mL of distilled water to a flask. Carefully add 0.68 mL of concentrated (14.8 M) ammonium hydroxide (NH_4OH). Stir to mix, then dilute to 100 mL with distilled water.

Hydrochloric Acid, 0.1 M: Add about 50 mL of distilled water to a flask. Carefully add 0.83 mL of concentrated (12.1 M) hydrochloric acid. Stir to mix, then dilute to 100 mL with distilled water. Remember: Always add acid to water.

Phenolphthalein, 0.5% in Alcohol: Add about 25 mL of 95% ethyl alcohol to a flask, followed by 0.25 g of phenolphthalein solid. Stir to dissolve and dilute to 50 mL with ethyl alcohol.

Sodium Hydroxide, 0.1 M: Add about 100 mL of distilled water to a flask. Carefully add 0.80 g of sodium hydroxide pellets and stir to dissolve. Dilute to 200 mL with distilled water.

Safety Precautions

All of the acids and bases used in this lab are corrosive to eyes, skin, and other body tissues. They are toxic by ingestion. Avoid contact of all chemicals with eyes and skin. Keep spill materials on hand to neutralize acids and bases in case of spills. Use sodium carbonate or sodium bicarbonate to neutralize acid solutions. Use citric acid to neutralize base spills. Magnesium metal is a flammable solid and burns with an intense flame. Keep away from flames. Phenolphthalein is an alcohol-based solution and is flammable. It is moderately toxic by ingestion. Keep away from flames and other ignition sources. Wear chemical splash goggles and chemical-resistant gloves and apron. Wash hands thoroughly with soap and water before leaving the laboratory. Please consult current Material Safety Data Sheets for additional safety, handling, and disposal information.

The concentrations of acetic acid, hydrochloric acid, and sodium hydroxide must be precise to two significant figures in order to obtain reliable results in the dropwise neutralization reactions in Part B. Use 1 mL serological pipets and volumetric flasks or prepare larger volumes. Alternatively, ready-made solutions may be purchased from Flinn Scientific.

Teacher's Notes

Disposal

Consult your current *Flinn Scientific Catalog/Reference Manual* for general guidelines and specific procedures governing the disposal of laboratory waste. All of the solutions may be flushed down the drain with excess water according to Flinn Suggested Disposal Method #26b. The used paper strips should be discarded in the solid waste disposal according to Flinn Suggested Disposal Method #26a. Unreacted metal pieces from Part A should be added to excess 1 M hydrochloric acid solution. The resulting solutions may be neutralized and flushed down the drain after the metal pieces have fully reacted.

Lab Hints

- This experiment is designed as a qualitative introduction to the properties of acids and bases. The experiment can reasonably be completed in one 50-minute lab period.

- Stagger the starting points for the different tests in Part A to accommodate the number of conductivity testers available in the classroom. A class of 30 students, working in pairs, should conveniently be able to share a set of 3–5 conductivity testers. If individual conductivity testers are not available, consider doing the conductivity tests as a demonstration using a traditional, lightbulb conductivity tester.

- Flinn conductivity meters (AP1493) are small-scale testers for individual student measurement of microscale quantities of solutions. The electrodes are about 2 cm long and are easily inserted into the wells on microscale reaction plates. Two LEDs make it possible to quantitatively compare the conductivity of solutions. The green LED requires more voltage than the red LED. A weak electrolyte will cause the red LED to glow, but not the green LED. A strong electrolyte will cause both the red and green LEDs to glow. A scale attached to the back of the meter allows solutions to be characterized as strong, moderate, weak, and nonelectrolytes. Because the meter uses only a 9-volt battery, it is convenient, portable, and safe.

- Litmus tests are often carried out using blue and red litmus paper to detect acids and bases, respectively. Neutral litmus paper, however, provides exactly the same information and uses only half the quantity of paper. Neutral litmus paper turns red in acid, blue in base.

- The concentrations of acids and bases in this experiment were intentionally kept low (0.1 M). The low concentrations make it possible to distinguish between strong versus weak acids or bases in the conductivity test and also give a range of pH values. Because the acid concentrations are low, however, the reactions with magnesium metal are less vigorous.

- The following demonstration can be used to identify the production of hydrogen gas in the metal reactions. Construct a gas generator using a small test tube, rubber stopper, and a graduated, Beral-type pipet. Cut the pipet as shown on the next page, construct the gas delivery tube, and fill the pipet bulb with water. Place 0.5 g of magnesium into the test tube and fill the test tube about ¾ full with 1 M hydrochloric acid. Replace the rubber stopper and collect the hydrogen gas by water displacement. To test for hydrogen, collect a pipet-bulb full of the gas, place a burning splint near the mouth of the pipet bulb, and quickly squeeze the bulb. A large pop will be heard and the flame will quickly extinguish.

The following schematic illustrates what the Flinn conductivity meter looks like and how it works.

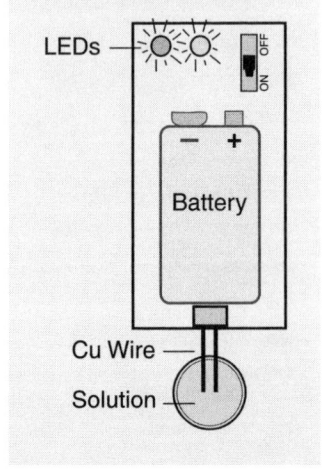

Teacher's Notes

Teacher Notes

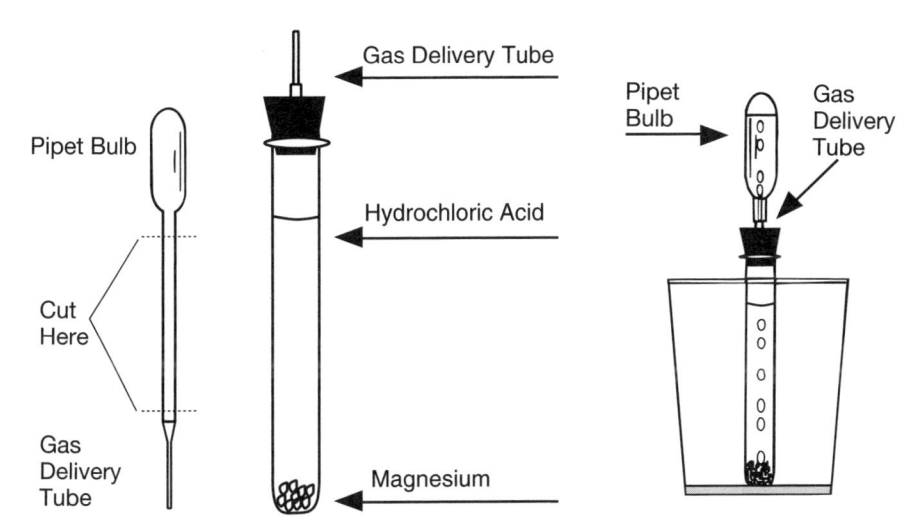

- This experiment can easily be adapted to an inquiry-based lab activity. The *Supplementary Information* section contains a set of questions that can be used as a working guide for students to study the properties of acids and bases.

Teaching Tips

- The focus of this experiment is observation and classification. Allowing students to develop their own working definitions of acids and bases is more effective than having them memorize the same definitions from a lecture or textbook. The goal of this empirical approach is not that student understanding of acids and bases should end with these working definitions. Rather, the goal is to give students a practical foundation before they move on to theory and calculations.

- The difference between strong and weak acids is frequently misunderstood by students, who may confuse strong acids with concentrated solutions and weak acids with dilute solutions. In order to avoid misunderstanding, the solutions in this experiment all had the same concentration. Strong and weak acids (or bases) can be distinguished by their pH values if the solutions all have the same concentration. If two acids have the same concentration, then a stronger acid solution will have a lower pH value than a weaker acid. Thus, 0.1 M hydrochloric acid has a pH of 1, 0.1 M acetic acid has a pH of 3, while 0.1 M para-nitrophenol would have a pH of about 4. If two bases have the same concentration, then a stronger base will have a higher pH value than a weaker base. Thus, 0.1 M sodium hydroxide has a pH of 13, 0.1 M ammonia has a pH of 11, while 0.1 M sodium bicarbonate would have a pH value of about 10.

- Another common student misconception concerns the meaning of the term neutral. In earlier discussions of elements and compounds, the term neutral has surely been used to describe uncharged atoms or molecules. In the context of acids and bases, however, the term neutral is used to describe substances that are neither acidic nor basic.

- A valuable extension of this lab would be to test the effect of concentration on the conductivity, pH, and neutralization of HCl. To do this, simply add 0.01 M HCl to the list of solutions in Part A.

The pH of any given acid also depends on its concentration, of course. To demonstrate this concept to your students, have them dilute the 0.1 M HCl solution by a factor of 10 (1 drop HCl plus 9 drops water) and measure the pH with test paper.

Properties of Acids and Bases

Teacher's Notes

Answers to Pre-Lab Questions *(Student answers will vary.)*

Acid wit, acid rain, and an acid test—these familiar expressions suggest some interesting properties and uses of acids.

1. The phrase *acid wit* is defined in the dictionary as humor that is sharp, biting, or sour in nature. In the laboratory, acids present a hazard because they are corrosive. What is meant by the term corrosive? How does this relate to acid wit?

   The term corrosive refers to substances that may irritate and burn body tissues, notably the skin and, when taken internally, the lungs and stomach. Corrosive substances such as acids will also attack and destroy many other kinds of materials, including metals and fabrics. Acid wit may also attack and destroy!

2. *Acid rain* is recognized as a growing danger to the environment. Briefly describe two problems associated with acid rain.

   Acid rain is dangerous to fish and wildlife by reducing fish populations in affected lakes and streams, for example. It also causes economic damage by reacting with and corroding man-made buildings and statues.

3. *(Optional)* The phrase *acid test* has entered the popular vocabulary to describe a severe but conclusive test of whether something is authentic. What is the origin of the term acid test?

   Note to teachers: *This is a hard question. The term acid test probably originated in the days of the Gold Rush. Suspect metals were treated with concentrated acid—base metals dissolve in concentrated acid, gold does not. Gold is, of course, considered a precious metal precisely because it is unreactive. A mixture of concentrated nitric and hydrochloric acids (aqua regia) is required to dissolve gold.*

Teacher's Notes

Teacher Notes

Sample Data

Student data will vary.

Data Table A. *Classifying Acids and Bases*

Test Property	Solution				
	1	2	3	4	5
	Hydrochloric Acid	Acetic Acid	Distilled Water	Ammonia	Sodium Hydroxide
Conductivity	Good conductor—both LEDs light up. Bubbles observed on negative electrode.	Poor conductor—only one LED lights up.	Non-conductor. No effect.	Poor conductor—only one LED lights up.	Good conductor—both LEDs light up. Bubbles observed on negative electrode.
Litmus Paper	Pink	Pink	No change	Blue	Blue
Phenolphthalein	Colorless	Colorless	Colorless	Pink	Red-violet
pH Test Paper	1	3	6–7	11	13
Universal Indicator	Red	Red	Green	Blue	Purple
Reaction with Magnesium	Rapid reaction. Solution bubbles and fizzes; metal corrodes slightly.	Moderate to slow reaction. Slow evolution of gas bubbles from metal surface.	NR	NR	NR

Data Table B. *Neutralization Reactions of Acids and Bases*

	Hydrochloric Acid	Acetic Acid
Number of Drops of Sodium Hydroxide Added (Trial 1)	20 drops	21 drops
Number of Drops of Sodium Hydroxide Added (Trial 2)	22 drops	19 drops

Very faint conductivity may be observed for the "pure" water control if deionized, rather than distilled, water is used. Deionized water is obtained by passing water through an ion-exchange column, which removes calcium ions by replacing them.

Properties of Acids and Bases

Teacher's Notes

Answers to Post-Lab Questions *(Student answers will vary.)*

1. Use the results of the conductivity test to identify each solution in Part A as a strong electrolyte, weak electrolyte, or nonelectrolyte.

   Hydrochloric acid and sodium hydroxide solutions are strong electrolytes and acetic acid and ammonia solutions are weak electrolytes. Distilled water is a non-electrolyte.

2. Which solutions in Part A reacted with magnesium metal? Write a balanced chemical equation for the reaction of each acid in Part A with magnesium.

   Hydrochloric acid and acetic acid both reacted with magnesium metal.
   $2HCl(aq) + Mg(s) \rightarrow MgCl_2(aq) + H_2(g)$
   $2CH_3COOH(aq) + Mg(s) \rightarrow Mg(CH_3COO)_2(aq) + H_2(g)$

3. *Strong acids* ionize completely in water to form ions and are thus strong electrolytes. In contrast, *weak acids* do not readily ionize in water—in fact, less than 1% of the molecules are probably ionized at any given time. Weak acids are therefore weak electrolytes. Classify each acid as either a strong or weak acid. Which reacted faster with magnesium metal, the strong acid or the weak acid?

   Hydrochloric acid is a strong acid; acetic acid is a weak acid. The strong acid reacted faster than the weak acid with magnesium.

4. Write chemical equations for ionization of the strong and weak acids in water. Identify the common ion that is produced in acidic solutions.

   $HCl(aq) + H_2O(l) \rightarrow Cl^-(aq) + H_3O^+(aq)$
   $CH_3COOH(aq) + H_2O(l) \rightarrow CH_3COO^-(aq) + H_3O^+(aq)$
   The common ion produced by these acids in water is H_3O^+.

5. How can litmus paper and phenolphthalein be used to tell whether a solution is an acid or a base? Be specific.

   Neutral litmus paper turns red in acidic solutions, blue in neutral or basic solutions. Phenolphthalein indicator is colorless in acidic or neutral solutions, pink or red-violet in basic solution.

6. Use the combined results of the conductivity and indicator tests to identify the basic solutions in Part A. Classify each as a *strong* versus *weak* base.

   Sodium hydroxide and ammonia are basic solutions. Sodium hydroxide is a strong electrolyte, and thus a strong base, while ammonia is a weak electrolyte and therefore a weak base.

7. Write chemical equations for the ion-forming reactions of the strong and weak bases in water. Identify the common ion that is produced in basic solutions.

   $NaOH(aq) \rightarrow Na^+(aq) + OH^-(aq)$
   $NH_3(aq) + H_2O(l) \rightarrow NH_4^+(aq) + OH^-(aq)$
   The common ion produced in basic solutions is OH^-.

Teacher Notes

The reactions of acetic acid and ammonia with water, as shown in Questions 4 and 7, respectively, are reversible and should be indicated by double arrows. At this stage, however, students would not be expected to know this. See the "Strong Acid, Weak Acid Chemical Demonstration" for an excellent demonstration of this principle.

Teacher Notes

8. Compare the pH data for the solutions which you labeled as acids and bases. What pH values can be assigned to acids and bases, respectively?

   Acidic solutions have pH values less than 7. Basic solutions have pH values greater than 7.

9. Compare the pH values of strong versus weak acid and strong versus weak base solutions. How does pH vary with the "strength" of an acid or base, respectively?

   If the concentrations of two acids are the same, a solution of a stronger acid will have a lower pH value than a solution of a weaker acid. Thus, the pH of 0.1 M hydrochloric acid is 1, while the pH of 0.1 M acetic acid is 3. If the concentrations of two bases are the same, a solution of a stronger base will have a higher pH value than a solution of a weaker base. Thus, the pH of 0.1 M sodium hydroxide is 13, while the pH of 0.1 M ammonia is 11.

10. Explain the color change observed for the indicator in the neutralization reaction of hydrochloric acid in Part B. What is the pH range of the final solution?

    The phenolphthalein indicator was initially colorless, as expected, in the acid solution, but turned red as base was added. At first the color disappeared with stirring, but addition of the final drop of base caused the solution to turn red and stay red. The pH of the final solution must therefore be in the basic range, or greater than 7. **Note to teacher:** *This may be confusing to students, since neutralization reactions are supposed to produce neutral solutions. Since the reactants and products are all colorless, an indicator must be added to produce a visible color change. Ideally, of course, the last drop just makes the solution basic.*

11. (a) Write separate, balanced equations for the neutralization reactions of hydrochloric acid and acetic acid with sodium hydroxide.

    $HCl(aq) + NaOH(aq) \rightarrow NaCl(aq) + H_2O(l)$

    $CH_3COOH(aq) + NaOH(aq) \rightarrow CH_3COONa(aq) + H_2O(l)$

    (b) Use the stoichiometry of the balanced chemical equations to explain the number of drops of sodium hydroxide required for complete neutralization of the acids.

    Reaction of 20 drops of either acid required almost exactly the same number (19–22) drops of sodium hydroxide for complete neutralization. This makes sense—according to the balanced chemical equations, one mole of either acid will react with one mole of sodium hydroxide to form a salt and water. Since all of the acid and base solutions have the same concentration (0.1 M), the predicted result is that 20 drops of acid should require exactly 20 drops of sodium hydroxide for neutralization. The small difference between the actual and predicted results is due to experimental error (differences in the size of the drops, in the precise molarity of the solutions, etc.) **Note to teacher:** *It may be helpful to discuss sources of experimental error and what kind of reproducibility (uncertainty) is reasonable, given the way the procedure is run. Remind students that equal volumes of solutions of equal concentration contain equal numbers of moles of reagents.*

Teacher's Notes

(c) Did the strong and weak acids require equal number of drops of sodium hydroxide? Explain.

Both the strong and weak acid required the same number of drops of sodium hydroxide (within experimental error). Although the weak acid is only partially ionized in aqueous solution, all of the weak acid molecules are capable of reacting with a strong base.

(d) Did adding water to the acid solutions change the number of drops of sodium hydroxide required for neutralization? Explain.

Adding water diluted the concentration of the acid but did not change the number of moles of acid that were present. Therefore, adding water did not change the number of drops of sodium hydroxide required for neutralization.

12. Complete the following table to summarize the properties of acids and bases.

Property	Acids	Bases
Conductivity	Strong or weak electrolytes	Strong or weak electrolytes
Litmus	Red	Blue
Phenolphthalein	Colorless	Red
Reaction with metals	Vigorous reaction evolves hydrogen gas	No reaction
pH	Less than 7	Greater than 7

Supplementary Information

This experiment may be adapted to an inquiry-based experiment by giving students the following questions to investigate. The materials required are the same as those provided in the student section of this write-up.

Investigating the Properties of Acids and Bases—Student Objectives

1. What happens when strong acids come into contact with active metals? (The adjective "active" describes an element that reacts readily with many other elements. Magnesium is an active metal.)

2. Are all acids and bases strong electrolytes? Does the conductivity of an acid depend on its concentration? What other factors appear to influence the conductivity of acids and bases?

3. Compare and contrast the effects of acids and bases on indicators. Study a variety of indicators with different acids and bases.

4. What happens to the color of an indicator if you start with a fixed amount of a strong acid and add strong base to it, one drop at a time?

Teacher Notes

Natural Indicators
Acids, Bases, and the pH Scale

Introduction

Roses are red, violets are blue—or are they? Red roses, as well as many other flowers and fruits, contain natural indicators that are sensitive to acids and bases. The color of a natural acid–base indicator depends on pH. One of the most well known effects of natural indicators in plants occurs in the hydrangea or snowball plant. Hydrangea flowers are blue when grown in acidic soils, pink or red in basic soils. How do the colors of natural indicators vary with pH?

Concepts

- Indicators
- Extraction
- pH Scale
- Weak acid
- Conjugate base
- Equilibrium

Background

Indicators are dyes or pigments that can be isolated from a variety of sources, including plants, fungi, and algae. Almost any flower, for example, that is red, blue, or purple in color contains a class of organic pigments called anthocyanins that change color with pH. The use of natural dyes as acid–base indicators was first reported in 1664 by Sir Robert Boyle in his collection of essays *Experimental History of Colours*. Indeed, Boyle made an important contribution to the early theory of acids and bases by using indicators for the experimental classification of these substances. The idea, however, may actually have originated much earlier—medieval painters used natural dyes treated with vinegar and limewater to make different color watercolor paints.

Acid–base indicators are large organic molecules that behave as weak acids—they can donate hydrogen ions to water molecules to form their conjugate bases (Equation 1). The distinguishing characteristic of indicators is that the acid (HIn) and conjugate base (In$^-$) forms are different colors.

$$HIn(aq) + H_2O(l) \rightleftharpoons In^-(aq) + H_3O^+(aq) \qquad \textit{Equation 1}$$
$$(\text{color A}) \qquad\qquad\qquad (\text{color B})$$

The abbreviation HIn represents an uncharged indicator molecule, and In$^-$ an indicator ion after it has lost a hydrogen ion. The color changes of acid–base indicators illustrate an application of reversible reactions and equilibrium. Because indicators are weak acids, the reactions summarized in Equation 1 are reversible. Reversible reactions can easily be forced to go in either direction, depending on reaction conditions. The actual color of an indicator solution thus reflects the position of equilibrium for Equation 1 and depends on the concentration of H_3O^+ ions (and hence the pH).

There are three possible cases. (1) Most of the indicator molecules exist in the form HIn and the color of the solution is essentially the color of HIn. (2) Most of the indicator molecules exist in the form In$^-$ and the color of the solution is essentially the color of In$^-$. (3) The solution contains roughly equal amounts of the two forms and the resulting color is intermediate between that of HIn and In$^-$. The exact concentrations of H_3O^+ at which cases 1–3 will

Natural Indicators

predominate depend on the structure of the indicator molecule and the equilibrium constant for Equation 1. Different indicators thus change color at different pH ranges.

Natural indicator solutions are obtained by treating flowers and fruits with a solvent to remove (dissolve) the soluble components. This process, called extraction, is similar to the procedure used to make a cup of tea using a tea bag. The solid is crushed or ground and extracted with an appropriate solvent, such as boiling water, ethyl alcohol, or rubbing alcohol.

The color of an acid–base indicator depends on the concentration of H_3O^+ ions, which is most conveniently expressed using the pH scale. The mathematical relationship between pH and $[H_3O^+]$ is given in Equation 2.

$$pH = -\log[H_3O^+] \qquad \text{Equation 2}$$

The H_3O^+ concentration in water ranges from 1 M (10^0) in 1 M hydrochloric acid to 10^{-14} M in 1 M sodium hydroxide. In pure water, which is neutral (neither acidic nor basic), the H_3O^+ concentration is equal to 10^{-7} M. The logarithm of the concentration is the "power of ten" exponent in these concentration terms. Thus, the negative logarithms (Equation 2) of typical H_3O^+ concentrations are positive numbers from 0–14. The pH scale ranges from 0–14, with 7 being neutral. Acids have pH values less than 7, while bases have pH values greater than 7.

Within the pH range of acid solutions, either a more concentrated or a strong acid solution will have a lower pH than a less concentrated or a weak acid solution, respectively. Thus, the pH values of 0.1 and 0.01 M HCl solutions are 1 and 2, respectively, while the pH of 0.1 M acetic acid is about 3. On the basic side of the pH scale, either a more concentrated or strong base solution will have a higher pH than a less concentrated or a weak base solution, respectively. Thus, the pH values of 0.1 and 0.01 M NaOH solutions are 13 and 12, respectively, while the pH of 0.1 M ammonia is about 11. Remember that the pH scale is logarithmic—a solution of pH 3 is ten times more acidic than a solution of pH 4, and 100 times more acidic than a solution of pH 5. Figure 1 summarizes the pH scale and the pH range of acids and bases.

0	1	2	3	4	5	6	7	8	9	10	11	12	13	14

Strong acids　　　Weak acids　　　Neutral　　　Weak bases　　　Strong bases

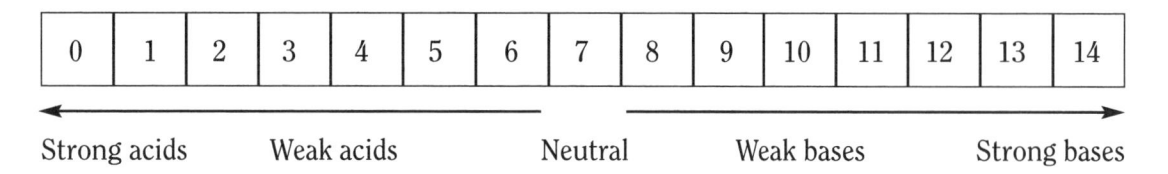

Figure 1. The pH Scale

Experiment Overview

The purpose of this experiment is to extract natural indicators from flowers and fruits and design a procedure to investigate their color changes as a function of pH. A set of standard acid and base solutions of known pH (pH = 2–12) will be provided. The results will be used to construct color charts of the indicators. In Part B, the natural indicators will be used, along with other known indicator solutions, to analyze the pH values of unknown solutions.

Teacher Notes

The pH scale, of course, is not restricted to integer values. The ease of use of scientific calculators has made it possible for students of varied math backgrounds to convert $[H_3O^+]$ concentration terms to pH values, and vice versa. Review with students how to use their calculators for these conversions.

Page 3 – **Natural Indicators**

Teacher Notes

Pre-Lab Questions

Phenolphthalein is a synthetic indicator that is colorless when the pH < 8 and red when the pH > 10. The pH range from 8–10 is the "transition range" for phenolphthalein. When phenolphthalein is added to solutions having a pH between 8 and 10, the indicator is intermediate in color between colorless and red, or various shades of pink. The color changes for phenolphthalein and two other indicators are summarized in the following *color charts* (Table 1). Areas shaded with hash marks indicate pH intervals in which the color of the indicator changes from one form to another. *Note:* Alizarin exhibits two different color transitions, between 5–7 and 11–13, respectively. At pH values greater than 12 alizarin appears violet.

Table 1.

Indicator	pH 1	2	3	4	5	6	7	8	9	10	11	12
Phenolphthalein	Colorless							///	///	Red		
Bromthymol Blue	Yellow					///	///	Blue				
Alizarin	Yellow			///	///	Red					///	///

1. What will be the intermediate color of bromthymol blue in a solution of pH 7?

2. A colorless household solution was tested with the three indicators shown above. The solution was colorless with phenolphthalein, yellow with bromthymol blue, and orange with alizarin. What is the pH of the solution? *Be as specific as possible.*

Materials

Standard acid and base solutions of known pH (pH 2–12), 5 mL each

Flowers or fruits (roses, violets, geraniums, pansies, petunias, peaches, cherries, cranberries, grapes, plums), about 5 g

Indicator solutions, 5 mL each
- Thymol blue
- Methyl orange
- Bromthymol blue

Isopropyl ("rubbing") alcohol, 50 mL

"Unknown" acids and bases, 5 mL each

Water, distilled or deionized

Beakers, 100- and 150-mL, 1 each

Color pencils, 1 set

Pipets, Beral-type, 5

Reaction plate, 24-well

Funnels and filter paper (optional)

Hot plate (optional)

Mortar and pestle (optional)

Safety Precautions

The standard acid and base solutions used in this experiment are body tissue irritants. Avoid contact of all chemicals with eyes and skin. Isopropyl alcohol is flammable. Keep away from flames and other ignition sources. Wear chemical splash goggles and chemical-resistant gloves and apron. Wash hands thoroughly with soap and water before leaving the laboratory.

Natural Indicators – Page 4

Procedure

Teacher Notes

Preparation. Extraction of Natural Indicators

1. Obtain about 5 g of flower petals or fruit skin. *Note:* For small fruits that are not easily peeled, use the entire fruit.

2. Tear, chop, grind, or crush the plant material and place the pieces in a 150-mL beaker.

3. Cover the sample with water or isopropyl alcohol. Use a minimum amount of solvent (approximately 50 mL).

4. If water is used as the solvent, heat the mixture to just below the boiling point using a hot plate or Bunsen burner setup. Do not heat the mixture if isopropyl alcohol is used.

5. After 15 minutes, decant or filter the mixture into a clean, 100-mL beaker. The indicator solution should be clear, not cloudy.

Part A. Indicator Color Changes

6. Design a procedure using the standard acid and base solutions of known pH to determine the color changes for the natural indicator solution and the pH intervals in which the color changes occur.

7. Construct a data table to record the results.

8. Show the data table and discuss the proposed procedure with your instructor.

9. Carry out the procedure and record the results.

Part B. Classifying Unknown Solutions

10. Design a procedure using your natural indicator solution and at least one other synthetic indicator to determine the pH values of unknown solutions. *Hint:* Choose indicators that will give you the narrowest range possible for the pH value of each unknown. The color charts for the available indicators are shown in Table 2.

11. Construct a data table to record the results.

12. Show your data table and discuss the proposed procedure with your instructor.

13. Carry out the procedure and record the results.

Table 2.

pH Value	0	1	2	3	4	5	6	7	8	9	10	11
Thymol Blue	Red			Yellow							Blue	
Methyl Orange	Red				Yellow							
Bromthymol Blue	Yellow							Blue				

The extraction time can be reduced by covering the plant material with alcohol and gently grinding it with the bottom of a test tube. It is usually possible to obtain a clear indicator extract by withdrawing the liquid into a Beral-type pipet, without first filtering the mixture.

Teacher Notes

Name: _____

Class/Lab Period: _____

Natural Indicators

Post-Lab Questions

1. Assume that the pH 2 color of the natural indicator represents its most acidic form (HIn).

    (a) What is the pH range in which the most acidic form predominates?

    (b) Calculate the *lowest* H_3O^+ concentration at which the indicator still exists in this form.

2. Assume that the pH 12 color of the natural indicator represents its most basic form (In$^-$).

    (a) What is the pH range in which the most basic form predominates?

    (b) Calculate the *highest* H_3O^+ concentration at which the indicator still exists in this form.

3. For one of the unknown acid–base solutions that you tested, explain why you chose the combination of indicators you did to determine the pH value of the solution. What is the advantage of using multiple indicators, rather than a single indicator, to determine the pH of a substance?

4. Construct a *Results Table* to summarize the properties of the unknowns.
    (a) Estimate the pH value of each unknown.
    (b) Classify each solution as acidic or basic.
    (c) Within each class of unknowns—acids and bases—arrange the solutions in order from least acidic to most acidic and least basic to most basic, respectively.

Teacher's Notes
Natural Indicators

Master Materials List *(for a class of 30 students working in pairs)*

Standard acid and base solutions of known pH (pH 2–12), 100 mL each*

Flowers and fruits (roses, violets, geraniums, pansies, petunias, peaches, cherries, cranberries, grapes, plums)

Indicator solutions, 100 mL each
   Thymol blue, 0.04%
   Methyl orange, 0.1%
   Bromthymol blue, 0.04%

Unknown acid–base solutions, 0.1 M, 100 mL each†
   Acetic acid, CH_3COOH
   Ammonia, NH_3
   Ammonium nitrate, NH_4NO_3
   Phosphoric acid, H_3PO_4
   Sodium bicarbonate, $NaHCO_3$
   Sodium phosphate, monobasic, NaH_2PO_4
   Zinc nitrate, $Zn(NO_3)_2$

Balances, centigram (.01 g precision), 3
Isopropyl ("rubbing") alcohol, 750 mL
Wash bottles and distilled or deionized water, 15
Hot plates (optional)
Color pencils, assorted, 15
Beakers, 100- and 150-mL, 15 each
Funnels and filter paper (optional), 15
Mortars and pestles (optional), 15
Pipets, Beral-type, 75
Reaction plates, 24-well, 15

*Buffer capsules (Flinn Catalog No. B0227) provide a convenient and inexpensive way to obtain standard solutions having pH values of 2–12, respectively. See the *Preparation of Solutions* section for a description of buffer capsules and their use.

†Label the unknowns with letter codes for student use. See also the *Supplementary Information* section for suggestions on using household substances as unknowns in Part B.

Preparation of Solutions *(for a class of 30 students working in pairs)*

Buffer Solutions, pH 2–12: Use buffer capsules to prepare standard acid–base solutions of known pH. Buffer capsules contain pre-weighed amounts of stable, dry powders that dissolve in water to give solutions of known, constant pH. Each capsule makes 100 mL of buffer solution. A set of buffer capsules is available that allows you to prepare 100 mL of each buffer solution in the pH range 2–12.

Indicator Solutions (for Part B)

Thymol Blue, 0.04%: To 50 mL of distilled or deionized water, add 0.04 g of thymol blue and 5 mL of 0.01 M sodium hydroxide solution. Stir to dissolve and dilute to 100 mL with distilled water.

Methyl Orange, 0.1%: Dissolve 0.1 g of methyl orange in 75 mL of distilled or deionized water, then dilute to 100 mL.

Bromthymol Blue, 0.04%: Dissolve 0.04 g of bromthymol blue in 50 mL of distilled or deionized water, then dilute to 100 mL.

Flowers and fruits do not have to be fresh. Dried flower petals also give good natural indicator extracts, as do canned fruits that are preserved in their "natural juices."

Teacher's Notes

Teacher Notes

Unknown Acid and Base Solutions (for Part B)

Phosphoric Acid, 0.1 M: Add 0.7 mL of concentrated phosphoric acid (14.8 M) to 50 mL of distilled or deionized water. Mix the solution and dilute to 100 mL with water.

Acetic Acid, 0.1 M: Add 0.6 mL of glacial acetic acid (17.4 M) to 50 mL of distilled or deionized water. Mix the solution and dilute to 100 mL.

Sodium Phosphate, Monobasic, 0.1 M: Dissolve 1.38 g of sodium phosphate monobasic monohydrate ($NaH_2PO_4 \cdot H_2O$) in 50 mL of distilled or deionized water, then dilute to 100 mL.

Zinc Nitrate, 0.1 M: Dissolve 3.0 g of zinc nitrate hexahydrate in 50 mL of distilled or deionized water, then dilute to 100 mL.

Ammonium Nitrate, 0.1 M: Dissolve 0.8 g of ammonium nitrate in 50 mL of distilled or deionized water, then dilute to 100 mL.

Sodium Bicarbonate, 0.1 M: Dissolve 0.84 g of sodium bicarbonate in 50 mL of distilled or deionized water, then dilute to 100 mL.

Ammonia (Ammonium Hydroxide) Solution, 0.1 M: Add 0.7 mL of concentrated (14.8 M) ammonium hydroxide (NH_4OH) to 50 mL of distilled or deionized water. Mix the solution and dilute to 100 mL with water.

Safety Precautions

The standard acid and base solutions used in this experiment are body tissue irritants. Avoid contact of all chemicals with eyes and skin. Isopropyl alcohol is flammable. Keep away from flames and other ignition sources. Wear chemical splash goggles and chemical-resistant gloves and apron. Wash hands thoroughly with soap and water before leaving the laboratory. Please consult current Material Safety Data Sheets for additional safety, handling, and disposal information.

Disposal

Consult your current *Flinn Scientific Catalog/Reference Manual* for general guidelines and specific procedures governing the disposal of laboratory waste. All of the solutions may be flushed down the drain with excess water according to Flinn Suggested Disposal Method #26b.

Lab Hints

- This experiment is designed as a fun, inquiry-based study of indicators and their uses. Students generally enjoy any kind of "natural product" chemistry and this lab is no exception. Because the experiment works well with a wide range of materials, it is possible to give students a great deal of freedom in choosing flowers and fruits to test. This approach usually gives students more pride and ownership of work. The experiment can reasonably be completed in one 50-minute lab period.

- The inquiry approach may not be suitable for every classroom with every group of students. The *Supplementary Information* section contains an alternative, step-by-step procedure, along with prepared data tables. To use the alternative procedure, simply substitute pages 27–29 for page 18 in the handout that you give the students.

Save valuable time and money by purchasing ready-made solutions from Flinn Scientific. See the Master Materials Guide on pages 94–96 for catalog numbers and amounts of all solutions

Natural Indicators

Teacher's Notes

- To allow more time for measuring the indicator color changes and testing unknowns, consider setting up the extraction the day before lab. The amount of preparation time (to measure the flower or fruit "parts," chop them up, and place them in a beaker with isopropyl alcohol) is minimal—15 minutes should be sufficient. Cover the beaker with Parafilm™ or plastic wrap and allow the extraction to take place overnight. On the day of lab, filter or decant the mixture and use the resulting indicator solution in Parts A and B. Alternatively, extraction of the indicator with hot water may be completed as a homework assignment.

- Flowers and fruits may be extracted with hot water, ethyl alcohol, or with 70% isopropyl (rubbing) alcohol. There was no difference in the color charts of natural indicator solutions obtained using these different solvents. In our experience, isopropyl alcohol proved most efficient in terms of set-up time and ease of use. Using isopropyl alcohol also makes it possible to carry out the extraction overnight, which may be a major advantage in terms of time. The chief disadvantage to the use of isopropyl alcohol, in addition to cost, is the odor. This may be a problem if the experiment will be performed by multiple lab sections in the same room on the same day. Isopropyl alcohol should only be used in a well-ventilated lab setting. The recommended minimum extraction time is about 15 minutes regardless of the solvent used.

- Although the extraction step may be the most enjoyable part of this lab for students, it does tend to get a little messy—again, especially if the experiment will be performed by multiple lab sections in the same room on the same day. Teachers may find it convenient to use "ready-made" natural indicator extracts. Concentrated fruit juices, which are available in non-refrigerated containers, work well. See the *Sample Data* section for examples and results. Herbal teas provide another convenient alternative. A concentrated natural indicator with distinctive color changes was obtained from a very strong tea infusion (two teabags steeped in 100 mL of hot water for 15 minutes). For example, Red Zinger™ brand herbal teas (black cherry, peach, cranberry apple and blackberry) all gave an indicator that was red at pH 1–4, golden tan at pH 5 and 6, and green at pH >7. Although these are all different flavors, the major ingredient in all of them is hibiscus, suggesting that this is the hibiscus indicator. The best results were obtained using the cranberry apple brand. See the *Sample Data* section for a summary of results.

- As mentioned above, a wide range of fruits and flowers contain natural acid–base indicators. The following table summarizes the information obtained from a brief literature survey. The list is not meant to be exhaustive, but rather to demonstrate the variety of options suitable for classroom study.

For a review of natural indicators isolated from fruits and vegetables, see "Edible Acid–Base Indicators" in Journal of Chemical Education, *April 1985, page 285.*

Teacher's Notes

Teacher Notes

Natural Fruit and Vegetable indicators	Natural Flower Indicators	Do Not Give Natural Indicators
Apple skin (red)	Dahlias	Daffodils
Beets	Daylilies	Daisies
Blueberries	Geraniums	Dandelions
Cabbage (red)	Hibiscus	Marigolds
Cherries	Hollyhocks	Mums (yellow)
Cranberries	Hydrangeas	
Grapes (red or purple)	Iris (blue)	
Onions (red)	Morning glories	
Peaches	Mums (purple)	
Plums	Pansies	
Radish skin	Peonies	
Rhubarb skin	Petunias	
Strawberries	Poppies	
Tomato leaves	Roses (red, pink)	
Turnip skin	Violets	

- Consider holding a "Measurement Fair" to have students analyze the acid–base properties of household substances using their natural indicators. The *Supplementary Information* section contains a list of household substances to consider as unknowns for Part B.

Teaching Tip

- This experiment reinforces key concepts and definitions in the chemistry of acids and bases. The behavior of natural indicators illustrates the definition of Brønsted acids (proton donors). Most natural indicators are further classified as weak acids (dissociate only partially in water and their reactions with water are reversible). The different colors observed for natural indicators thus reflect the position of equilibrium under different conditions. The color transitions are examples of LeChâtelier's Principle in action. Use Equation 1 to predict the direction the indicator equilibrium will be shifted as a result of increasing or decreasing the H_3O^+ concentration. The *PostLab Questions* provide an opportunity to review the relationship between pH and $[H_3O^+]$ in pH calculations.

Natural Indicators

Teacher's Notes

Answers to Pre-Lab Questions *(Student answers will vary.)*

Phenolphthalein is a synthetic indicator that is colorless when the pH <8 and red when the pH >10. The pH range from 8–10 is the "transition range" for phenolphthalein. When phenolphthalein is added to solutions having a pH between 8 and 10, the indicator is intermediate in color between colorless and red, or various shades of pink. The color changes for phenolphthalein and two other indicators are summarized in the following *color charts* (Table 1). Areas shaded with hash marks indicate pH intervals in which the color of the indicator changes from one form to another. *Note:* Alizarin exhibits two different color transitions, between 5–7 and 11–13, respectively. At pH values greater than 12 alizarin appears violet.

Table 1.

Indicator	pH 1	2	3	4	5	6	7	8	9	10	11	12
Phenolphthalein	Colorless							*(transition)*		Red		
Bromthymol Blue	Yellow					*(transition)*		Blue				
Alizarin	Yellow				*(transition)*		Red			*(transition)*		

1. What will be the intermediate color of bromthymol blue in a solution of pH 7?

   The color should be intermediate between yellow and blue—green.

2. A colorless household solution was tested with the three indicators shown above. The solution was colorless with phenolphthalein, yellow with bromthymol blue, and orange with alizarin. What is the pH of the solution? *Be as specific as possible.*

   The pH ranges suggested by the indicator colors are pH <8 (phenolphthalein), pH <6 (bromthymol blue), and pH = 5–7 (alizarin). Combining these ranges gives a pH value between 5 and 6. The pH may be reported as the middle of this interval, with a "plus-or-minus" value to indicate the range: pH = 5.5 ±0.5.

Teacher Notes

Sample Data

Student data will vary.

Data Table A. *Indicator Color Changes*

Indicator Source	Roses (Red)	Mums (Purple)	Apples (Red)	Radishes	Grape Juice	Cherry Juice
Color of Extract	Purple	Purple	Red	Red	Purple	Red
Color Changes as a Function of pH						
pH 2	Dark pink	Pink	Dark pink	Peach	Dark pink	Coral pink
pH 3	Pink	Pink	Pink	Dark pink	Dark pink	Peach
pH 4	Pink	Pink	Light pink	Pink	Dark pink	Peach
pH 5	Light pink	Light pink	Pale pink	Pink	Pink	Pale peach
pH 6	Pale pink–colorless	Pale pink–colorless	Pale pink–colorless	Pink	Pink	Pale peach
pH 7	Colorless	Colorless	Pale yellow	Lavender	Lavender	Yellow
pH 8	Light green	Pale green	Pale yellow	Lavender	Lavender-green	Yellow
pH 9	Light green	Light green	Yellow-green	Light green	Lavender-green	Green
pH 10	Yellow	Yellow-green	Yellow-green	Light green	Green	Green
pH 11	Yellow	Yellow	Yellow-green	Yellow-green	Green	Green
pH 12	Yellow-gold	Yellow	Yellow	Yellow	Green	Green

Data Table B. *Classifying Unknown Solutions*

Unknown Solution	Identity*	Natural Indicator Red Rose	pH	Synthetic Indicator Identity	Color	pH
A	0.1 M H_3PO_4	Dark pink	≤ 2	Thymol blue	Red orange	1–2
B	0.1 M CH_3COOH	Pink	3–4	Methyl orange	Peach	3–4
C	0.1 M NaH_2PO_4	Light pink	5–6	Bromthymol blue	Yellow	≤ 5
D	0.1 M $Zn(NO_3)_2$	Pale pink	5–6	Bromthymol blue	Yellow green	6–7
E	0.1 M NH_4NO_3	Pale pink–colorless	6–7	Bromthymol blue	Yellow green	6–7
F	0.1 M NH_3	Yellow-gold	11–12	Thymol blue	Blue	10–11
G	0.1 M $NaHCO_3$	Light green	8–9	Thymol blue	Green	8–9

*Do not reveal the identity of the unknowns to the students.

A picture is worth a thousand words! Have students draw color charts of indicator color changes using colored pencils. Visit the Flinn website at www.flinnsci.com for photos of several natural indicator color changes.

Natural Indicators

Teacher's Notes

Answers to Post-Lab Questions *(Student answers will vary.)*

1. Assume that the pH 2 color of the natural indicator represents its most acidic form (HIn).

    (a) What is the pH range in which the most acidic form predominates?

    (b) Calculate the *lowest* H_3O^+ concentration at which the indicator still exists in this form.

    For the red rose indicator as an example, the most acidic form of the indicator is pink in color. This acidic form of the indicator appears to be the predominant form of the indicator in solution at pH values less than or equal to 4. The lowest H_3O^+ concentration at which the acidic form predominates is therefore 1×10^{-4} M. **Note to teacher:** *At pH 5–6, the solution is still pink, but it becomes very pale in color, and finally almost colorless at pH 7. The very pale pink color thus appears to be a "transition" or intermediate color.*

2. Assume that the pH 12 color of the natural indicator represents its most basic form (In⁻).

    (a) What is the pH range in which the most basic form predominates?

    (b) Calculate the *highest* H_3O^+ concentration at which the indicator still exists in this form.

    For the red rose indicator as an example, the most basic form of the indicator is yellow in color. This basic form of the indicator appears to be the predominant form of the indicator in solution at pH values greater than or equal to 10. The highest H_3O^+ concentration at which the basic form predominates is therefore 1×10^{-10} M.

3. For one of the unknown acid–base solutions that you tested, explain why you chose the combination of indicators you did to determine the pH value of the solution. What is the advantage of using multiple indicators, rather than a single indicator, to determine the pH of a substance?

    In the case of Unknown D (zinc nitrate), the natural red rose indicator gave a pH estimate of 5–6. Bromthymol blue was selected as an alternate indicator to confirm or narrow the pH range. Bromthymol blue was yellow green (the intermediate or transition color for this indicator), suggesting that the pH was in the 6–7 range. The overlap of these two pH estimates suggests that the pH of the solution is very close to 6. Using multiple indicators, rather than a single indicator, often makes it possible to obtain a more precise (narrow) estimate of the pH of a substance.

4. Construct a *Results Table* to summarize the properties of the unknowns.
    (a) Estimate the pH value of each unknown.
    (b) Classify each solution as acidic or basic.
    (c) Within each class of unknowns—acids and bases—arrange the solutions in order from least acidic to most acidic and least basic to most basic, respectively.

    See the Sample Results Table on page 27.

Teacher Notes

Flinn ChemTopic® Labs — Acids and Bases

Teacher's Notes

Teacher Notes

Sample Results Table

Acids			Bases	
Unknown	**pH**		**Unknown**	**pH**
H_3PO_4 (A)	1–2		$NaHCO_3$ (G)	8–9
CH_3COOH (B)	3		NH_3 (F)	11
NaH_2PO_4 (C)	5			
$Zn(NO_3)_2$ (D)	6			
NH_4NO_3 (E)	6–7			

(acidity increases ↑, basicity increases ↓)

Supplementary Information

Student Procedure

1. Obtain about 5 g of flower petals or fruit skin. *Note:* For small fruits that are not easily peeled, use the entire fruit.

2. Tear, chop, grind, or crush the plant material and place the pieces in a 150-mL beaker.

3. Cover the sample with water or isopropyl alcohol. Use a minimum amount of solvent (approximately 50 mL) so that the resulting indicator solution will be as concentrated as possible.

4. If water is used as the solvent, heat the mixture to just below the boiling point using a hot plate or Bunsen burner setup. Do not heat the mixture if isopropyl alcohol is used as the solvent.

5. After 15 minutes, decant or filter the mixture into a clean, 100-mL beaker. The natural indicator extract should be clear, not cloudy.

Part A. Indicator Color Changes

6. Using a pipet, add 20 drops (1 mL) of each standard acid and base solution (pH 2–12) to separate wells on a 24-well reaction plate. Note the location of each solution.

7. Add 5 drops of the natural indicator solution to each well.

8. Record the color of the indicator in each "standard" well in Data Table A.

9. Do NOT discard the solutions in the standard wells until steps 10–19 have been completed.

Teacher's Notes

Part B. Classifying Unknown Solutions

10. Using a pipet, add 20 drops (about 1 mL) of each unknown solution to be tested to a separate well on the 24-well reaction plate. Note the location of each solution.

11. Add 5 drops of the natural indicator to each well.

12. Record the color of the indicator in each "unknown" well in Data Table B.

13. Compare the color of each unknown to the colors of the indicator in the standard wells. Determine the pH of the standard solution that most closely matches the color of each unknown. *Note:* If the color of the indicator is the same in two or more standard wells, for example pH 2, 3, and 4, then find the pH range that most closely matches the color of the unknown.

14. Record the approximate pH value or pH range for each unknown in Data Table B.

Measure the pH of the unknowns using synthetic indicators:

15. Based on the approximate pH value or pH range for each unknown (Step 14), choose at least one indicator from the following table that will allow you either to narrow down the pH range or to confirm the pH value. *For example:* If the approximate pH range of an unknown is less than 4, choose thymol blue to narrow down the pH range.

pH Value	0	1	2	3	4	5	6	7	8	9	10	11
Thymol Blue	Red			Yellow							Blue	
Methyl Orange		Red				Yellow						
Bromthymol Blue		Yellow						Blue				

16. Record the indicator selected for each unknown in Data Table B.

17. Add 20 drops (1 mL) of each unknown to separate wells on the reaction plate.

18. Add 2 drops of the appropriate indicator to the test well of each unknown.

19. Record the color of each solution in Data Table B.

20. The contents of the reaction plate may be rinsed down the drain with excess water.

Teacher Notes

Teacher's Notes

Supplementary Information

Data Table A. *Indicator Color Changes*

Indicator Source	
Color of Extract	
Indicator Color Changes	
pH 2	
pH 3	
pH 4	
pH 5	
pH 6	
pH 7	
pH 8	
pH 9	
pH 10	
pH 11	
pH 12	

Data Table B. *Classifying Unknown Solutions*

Unknown Solution	Natural Indicator		Synthetic Indicator		
	Color	pH	Indicator Used	Color	pH
A					
B					
C					
D					
E					
F					
G					

Natural Indicators

Teacher's Notes

Supplementary Information

Analysis of Household Substances

The following household substances provide convenient unknowns for classifying acid–base solutions using indicators.

Alka-Seltzer®	Grapefruit juice
Ammonia, household	Hair spray
Antacid tablet	Hand lotion
Aspirin tablet	Laundry detergent
Baking powder	Lemon-lime soda
Baking soda	Lemon juice
Bleach	Milk
Club soda	Mouthwash
Cola	Shampoo
Contact lens solution	Tea
Cream of tartar	Toothpaste
Drain cleaning solution	Vinegar
Fruit Fresh®	Vitamin C tablet
Ginger ale	Windex®

Page 1 – **Measuring Acid Strength**

Teacher Notes

Measuring Acid Strength
K_a Values of Weak Acids

Introduction

Acids vary greatly in their strength—their ability to ionize or produce ions when dissolved in water. What factors determine the strength of an acid? In this experiment, the strength of acids will be measured by determining the equilibrium constants for their ionization reactions in water.

Concepts

- Weak acid
- Conjugate base
- Equilibrium constant
- Neutralization reaction

Background

The modern Brønsted definition of an acid relies on its ability to donate hydrogen ions to other substances. When an acid dissolves in water, it donates hydrogen ions to water molecules to form H_3O^+ ions. The general form of this reaction, called an ionization reaction, is shown in Equation 1, where HA is the acid and A^- its conjugate base after loss of a hydrogen ion. The double arrows represent a reversible reaction.

$$HA(aq) + H_2O(l) \rightleftharpoons A^-(aq) + H_3O^+(aq) \qquad \textit{Equation 1}$$

The equilibrium constant expression (K_a) for the reversible ionization of an acid is given in Equation 2. The square brackets refer to the molar concentrations of the reactants and products.

$$K_a = \frac{[A^-][H_3O^+]}{[HA]} \qquad \textit{Equation 2}$$

Not all acids, of course, are created equal. The strength of an acid depends on the value of its equilibrium constant K_a for Equation 1. Strong acids ionize completely in aqueous solution. The value of K_a for a strong acid is extremely large and Equation 1 essentially goes to completion—only H_3O^+ and A^- are present in solution. Weak acids, in contrast, ionize only partially in aqueous solution. The value of K_a for a weak acid is much less than one and Equation 1 is reversible—all species (HA, A^-, and H_3O^+) are present at equilibrium.

Polyprotic acids contain more than one ionizable hydrogen. Ionization of a polyprotic acid occurs in a stepwise manner, where each step is characterized by its own equilibrium constant (K_{a1}, K_{a2}, etc.). The second reaction (removal of the second acidic hydrogen) always occurs to a much smaller extent than the first reaction, and so K_{a2} is always significantly smaller than K_{a1}. Sulfuric acid (H_2SO_4) and phosphoric acid (H_3PO_4) are examples of polyprotic acids.

$$H_2A(aq) + H_2O(l) \rightleftharpoons HA^-(aq) + H_3O^+(aq) \qquad K_{a1} = \frac{[HA^-][H_3O^+]}{[H_2A]}$$

$$HA^-(aq) + H_2O(l) \rightleftharpoons A^{2-}(aq) + H_3O^+(aq) \qquad K_{a2} = \frac{[A^{2-}][H_3O^+]}{[HA^-]}$$

The concept of acid strength, as opposed to acid concentration and pH, is often poorly understood by students. This experiment provides a convincing demonstration of the relationship between the strength of a weak acid and its equilibrium constant.

Measuring Acid Strength

Measuring Acid Strength – Page 2

The ionization constant of a weak acid can be determined experimentally by measuring the H_3O^+ concentration in a dilute aqueous solution of the weak acid. This procedure is most accurate when the solution contains equal molar amounts of the weak acid and its conjugate base. Consider acetic acid as an example. Acetic acid (CH_3COOH) and the acetate anion (CH_3COO^-) represent a conjugate acid–base pair. The equilibrium constant expression for ionization of acetic acid is shown in Equation 3. If the concentrations of acetic acid and acetate ion are equal, then these two terms cancel out in the equilibrium constant expression, and Equation 3 reduces to Equation 4.

$$K_a = \frac{[CH_3COO^-][H_3O^+]}{[CH_3COOH]} \qquad \text{Equation 3}$$

$$K_a = [H_3O^+] \qquad \text{Equation 4}$$

In this experiment, solutions will be prepared in which the molar concentrations of an unknown acid and its conjugate base are equal. The pH of these solutions will then equal the pK_a for the acid. The definition of pK_a is closely related to that of pH. Thus, $pH = -\log[H_3O^+]$ and $pK_a = -\log K_a$. The substances that will be tested are salts of polyprotic acids that still contain an ionizable hydrogen. Sodium bisulfate, for example, is a weak acid salt; it contains Na^+ and HSO_4^- ions. The HSO_4^- ion is a weak acid—the equilibrium constant for ionization of HSO_4^- corresponds to K_{a2} for sulfuric acid.

$$H_2SO_4(aq) + H_2O(l) \rightleftharpoons HSO_4^-(aq) + H_3O^+(aq) \qquad K_{a1} = \frac{[HSO_4^-][H_3O^+]}{[H_2SO_4]}$$

$$HSO_4^-(aq) + H_2O(l) \rightleftharpoons SO_4^{2-}(aq) + H_3O^+(aq) \qquad K_{a2} = \frac{[SO_4^{2-}][H_3O^+]}{[HSO_4^-]}$$

Experiment Overview

The purpose of this experiment is to measure the pK_a value for ionization of an unknown weak acid. Solutions containing equal molar amounts of the weak acid and its conjugate base will be prepared by "half-neutralization" of the acid. Their pH values will then be measured and used to calculate the pK_a value for the unknown and determine its identity.

Pre-Lab Questions *(Use a separate sheet of paper to answer the following questions.)*

Phosphoric acid is a triprotic acid (three ionizable hydrogens). The values of its stepwise ionization constants are $K_{a1} = 7.5 \times 10^{-3}$, $K_{a2} = 6.2 \times 10^{-8}$, and $K_{a3} = 4.2 \times 10^{-13}$.

1. Write the chemical equation for the first ionization of phosphoric acid with water.

2. Write the equilibrium constant expression (K_{a1}) for this reaction.

3. What would be the pH of a solution when $[H_3PO_4] = [H_2PO_4^-]$?
   Note: $pH = -\log[H_3O^+]$.

*Page 3 – **Measuring Acid Strength***

Teacher Notes

4. *(Optional)* Phenolphthalein would not be an appropriate indicator to use to determine K_{a1} for phosphoric acid. Why not? Choose a suitable indicator from the following color chart.

Indicator	pH										
	1	2	3	4	5	6	7	8	9	10	11
Phenolphthalein	Colorless								Pink		Red
Methyl Red	Red				Orange		Yellow				
Orange IV	Orange		Peach	Yellow							

Materials

Unknown weak acids, about 0.5 g each
Phenolphthalein solution, 0.5%, 1 mL
Sodium hydroxide solution, NaOH, 0.1 M, 15 mL
Wash bottle and distilled or deionized water
pH Meter
Weighing dishes, 2
Balance, centigram (0.01 g precision)
Beaker, 150-mL, 1
Erlenmeyer flask, 125-mL
Graduated cylinder, 50- or 100-mL
Pipets, Beral-type, 2
Stirring rod

Safety Precautions

Acids and bases are skin and eye irritants. Avoid contact of all chemical with eyes and skin. Inform the teacher and clean up all acid and base spills immediately. Phenolphthalein is an alcohol-based solution and is flammable. Keep the solution away from flames. Wear chemical splash goggles and chemical-resistant gloves and apron. Wash hands thoroughly with soap and water before leaving the laboratory.

Procedure

1. Label two weighing dishes #1 and #2.
2. Obtain an unknown weak acid and record the unknown number in the data table.
3. Measure out a small quantity (0.15–0.20 g) of the unknown into each weighing dish. *Note:* It is not necessary to know the exact mass of each sample.
4. Using a graduated cylinder, measure precisely 50.0 mL of distilled water into a 150-mL beaker.
5. Transfer sample #1 to the water in the beaker and stir to dissolve.
6. Using a graduated cylinder, transfer precisely 25.0 mL of this acid solution into an Erlenmeyer flask.
7. Add 3 drops of phenolphthalein solution to the acid solution in the Erlenmeyer flask.
8. Using a Beral-type pipet, add sodium hydroxide solution dropwise to the flask. Gently swirl the flask while adding the sodium hydroxide solution.

The number of drops of base required in steps 8 and 9 depends on the mass of salt and its molecular weight. Although it is not necessary to know the exact number of drops added, it may be helpful for students to keep track of the general amount added (every 10 drops, for instance). This may help avoid frustration, especially if students make a mistake in the procedure.

Measuring Acid Strength – Page 4

9. Continue adding sodium hydroxide dropwise and swirling the solution until a faint pink color persists throughout the solution for at least 5 seconds. This is called the endpoint. *Note:* A pink color develops immediately when the base is added, but fades quickly once the solution is swirled. When nearing the endpoint, the pink color begins to fade more slowly. Proceed cautiously when nearing the endpoint, so as not to "overshoot" it.

At this point the solution in the beaker contains exactly one-half of the original amount of acid, essentially all of which is in the acid form, HA. The Erlenmeyer flask contains an equal amount of the conjugate base A^- obtained by neutralization.

10. Pour the contents of the flask back into the beaker. Pour the solution back and forth a few times to mix. *Note:* It is important to transfer the solution as completely as possible from the flask back into the beaker.

11. Using a pH meter, measure the pH of the resulting solution in the beaker, which contains equal molar amounts of the acid and its conjugate base. Record the pH in the data table.

12. Dispose of the beaker contents down the drain and rinse both the beaker and the Erlenmeyer flask with distilled water. Dry the beaker with a paper towel.

13. Repeat steps 4–12 using sample #2.

Teacher Notes

This is an excellent experiment for incorporating technology into the curriculum. Use a LabPro or CBL-2 to measure pH.

Teacher Notes

Name: _____

Class/Lab Period: _____

Measuring Acid Strength

Data Table.

Unknown Label	
Trial	pH
Sample #1	
Sample #2	

Post-Lab Questions *(Use a separate sheet of paper to answer the following questions.)*

1. Average the pH readings for each trial (samples #1 and 2) to calculate the average pK_a value for your unknown weak acid.

2. Comment on the precision (reproducibility) of the pK_a determinations. Describe sources of experimental error and their likely effect on the measured pK_a (pH) values.

3. The following table lists the identities of the possible unknowns in this experiment. Complete the table by calculating the pK_a value for each acid. *Note:* $pK_a = -\log K_a$.

Acid	Formula	K_a	pK_a
Potassium dihydrogen phosphate	KH_2PO_4	K_{a2} of $H_3PO_4 = 6.2 \times 10^{-8}$	
Potassium hydrogen sulfate	$KHSO_4$	K_{a2} of $H_2SO_4 = 1.2 \times 10^{-2}$	
Potassium hydrogen phthalate	$KHC_8H_4O_4$	K_{a2} of $H_2C_8H_4O_4 = 3.9 \times 10^{-6}$	
Potassium hydrogen tartrate	$KHC_4H_4O_6$	K_{a2} of $H_2C_4H_4O_6 = 4.6 \times 10^{-5}$	

4. Compare the pK_a value for your unknown with the information in the table. Determine the probable identity of the unknown.

5. Write separate equations for the unknown dissolving in water and for the ionization reaction of the weak acid anion that this salt contains.

6. Why was it not necessary to know the exact mass of each acid sample?

7. Why was it not necessary to know the exact concentration of the sodium hydroxide solution?

8. Why was it necessary to measure the exact volume of distilled water used to dissolve the acid, as well as the exact volume of solution transferred from the beaker to the Erlenmeyer flask?

Students may generally be familiar with the structures of the inorganic acid salts KH_2PO_4 and $KHSO_4$. They will be less familiar with the organic salts—even the pronunciations ("thal-ate" for phthalate) are unusual. In particular, students may question why one H atom stands out from the rest and is acidic. If possible, draw the structures of the phthalate and tartrate ions to illustrate the acidic H atom in each.

Teacher's Notes
Measuring Acid Strength

Master Materials List *(for a class of 30 students working in pairs)*

Unknown weak acid salts, about 3 g each*

    Potassium dihydrogen phosphate (potassium phosphate, monobasic), KH_2PO_4

    Potassium hydrogen sulfate (potassium bisulfate), $KHSO_4$

    Potassium hydrogen phthalate, $KHC_8H_4O_4$

    Potassium hydrogen tartrate (potassium bitartrate), $KHC_4H_4O_6$

Phenolphthalein solution, 0.5%, 25 mL	Balances, centigram (0.01 g precision), 3
Sodium hydroxide, NaOH, 0.1 M, 300 mL	Beakers, 150-mL, 15
Wash bottles and distilled or deionized water, 15	Erlenmeyer flasks, 125-mL, 15
pH Meters, 15	Graduated cylinders, 100-mL, 15
Stirring rods, 15	Pipets, Beral-type, 30
Weighing dishes, 30	Buffer solutions, pH 4 and 7, 100 mL each†

*Sodium salts have the same pK_a values as the potassium salts, but they will require slightly more sodium hydroxide for neutralization.

†For best results, calibrate the pH meters using standard pH 4 and 7 buffer solutions before use.

Preparation of Solutions *(for a class of 30 students working in pairs)*

Sodium Hydroxide, 0.1 M: Add 2.0 g of sodium hydroxide pellets to 250 mL of distilled or deionized water. Stir to dissolve and dilute to 500 mL with water. Sodium hydroxide solution will gradually absorb carbon dioxide from the air to form sodium carbonate. For best results, store in a plastic container and prepare within one week of use.

Safety Precautions

Acids and bases are skin and eye irritants. Avoid contact of all chemical with eyes and skin. Inform the teacher and clean up all acid and base spills immediately. Phenolphthalein is an alcohol-based solution and is flammable. Keep the solution away from flames. Wear chemical splash goggles and chemical-resistant gloves and apron. Wash hands thoroughly with soap and water before leaving the laboratory. Keep sodium bicarbonate and citric acid on hand to clean up acid and base spills, respectively. Please consult current Material Safety Data Sheets for additional safety, handling, and disposal information.

Disposal

Consult your current *Flinn Scientific Catalog/Reference Manual* for general guidelines and specific procedures governing the disposal of laboratory waste. All of the solutions may be flushed down the drain with excess water according to Flinn Suggested Disposal Method #26b.

Flinn pH meters (Catalog No. AP8673) are "individual" pH meters that provide an inexpensive and convenient way for an entire class to measure pH simultaneously.

Teacher's Notes

Teacher Notes

Lab Hints

- This experiment is designed to provide a quick measure of the ionization constants of weak acids. The procedure is elegant in its simplicity and provides excellent results. The actual lab work for this experiment may reasonably be completed in one 50-minute lab period.

- The experiment has been written with the intention of having students identify unknowns from a list of possibilities. Alternatively, the identities of the samples may be revealed to students and students may be asked to calculate K_a values and percent errors. The logarithmic scale of pK_a values tends to obscure fairly large percent errors in K_a determinations. Thus, the experimentally determined pK_a value of KH_2PO_4 (7.0) compares favorably with the literature value (7.2). The percent error in the corresponding K_a values—1.0×10^{-7} and 6.2×10^{-8} for the experimental and literature values, respectively—is quite large (38%).

- For best results, it is necessary that all solids be completely dissolved before performing the "half-neutralization" reactions with sodium hydroxide and that the solutions be thoroughly mixed at every stage. When the sodium hydroxide is added to neutralize the acid, the flask should be constantly swirled to mix the solutions. The addition of sodium hydroxide should stop when the phenolphthalein indicator just remains pink throughout the solution. Remind students to be careful not to overshoot the endpoint.

- The number of drops of sodium hydroxide required for "half-neutralization" of the unknowns varies from about 75 to 150 drops, depending on the the mass of salt used and the molar mass of the unknown. For best results, keep the mass of salt used less than 0.20 g.

- Technically, the pK_a of an acid may be determined by measuring the pH value in any solution of a weak acid of known concentration if the concentration of its conjugate base is also known. Many factors, especially dissolved carbon dioxide, may interfere with the accuracy of measurements. Under certain conditions the pH of a weak acid may be very sensitive to small changes in the concentrations of the weak acid and conjugate base. In practical terms, therefore, this procedure is most convenient when the solution contains equal molar amounts of the weak acid and its conjugate base—that is, when the solution is an ideal buffer.

- A buffer is any solution that contains appreciable amounts of both HA and A$^-$. By definition, the pH of a buffer is relatively insensitive to the addition of small amounts of strong acids and bases. The properties of a buffer are easily understood by looking at the titration curve (graph of pH versus equivalents of base added) for a weak acid. The titration curve is relatively flat in the "buffer region" (around the midpoint in the titration curve) corresponding to half-neutralization of the weak acid.

Teaching Tip

- Although the procedure for this experiment is straightforward, the concepts are challenging. Students must be able to write equilibrium constant expressions for acids and understand the mathematical relationship between pH measurements and H_3O^+ concentrations. They should also be familiar with the properties of diprotic acids and the nature of an "acid salt" of a diprotic acid.

Teacher's Notes

Answers to Pre-Lab Questions *(Student answers will vary.)*

Phosphoric acid is a triprotic acid (three ionizable hydrogens). The values of its stepwise ionization constants are $K_{a1} = 7.5 \times 10^{-3}$, $K_{a2} = 6.2 \times 10^{-8}$, and $K_{a3} = 4.2 \times 10^{-13}$.

1. Write the chemical equation for the first ionization of phosphoric acid with water.

$$H_3PO_4 + H_2O \rightleftharpoons H_2PO_4^- + H_3O^+$$

2. Write the equilibrium constant expression (K_{a1}) for this reaction.

$$K_{a1} = \frac{[H_2PO_4^-][H_3O^+]}{[H_3PO_4]}$$

3. What would be the pH of a solution when $[H_3PO_4] = [H_2PO_4^-]$? *Note:* $pH = -\log[H_3O^+]$.

When $[H_3PO_4] = [H_2PO_4^-]$, the hydrogen ion concentration is equal to K_{a1}.

$[H_3O^+] = K_{a1} = 7.5 \times 10^{-3}$

$pH = -\log[H_3O^+] = -\log(7.5 \times 10^{-3}) = -(-2.12) = 2.12$

Note to teacher: *Unless rigorous precautions are taken, pH measurements are only precise to one decimal place. In terms of significant figures, however, both decimal places are allowed in the pH calculation, because the first digit (**2**.12) corresponds to the exponent.*

4. *(Optional)* Phenolphthalein would not be an appropriate indicator to use to determine K_{a1} for phosphoric acid. Why not? Choose a suitable indicator from the following color chart.

Indicator	pH										
	1	2	3	4	5	6	7	8	9	10	11
Phenolphthalein	Colorless								Pink		Red	
Methyl Red		Red				Orange		Yellow			
Orange IV	Orange		Peach		Yellow						

The color change for phenolphthalein occurs between 8 and 10. This is significantly higher than the pH value for neutralization of only the first acidic hydrogen in H_3PO_4. At a pH of 10, in fact, almost 100% of the phosphoric acid initially present would be converted to HPO_4^{2-}.

Note to teacher: *In general, for the conversion of an acid HA to its conjugate base A^-, 99% of the compound will exist in the form A^- when the pH is 2 units higher than the pK_a value. Thus, in order to obtain complete conversion of H_3PO_4 to $H_2PO_4^-$, and avoid conversion of $H_2PO_4^-$ to HPO_4^{2-}, a pH range between 4 and 6 would be optimal. The orange transition color of methyl red would be a suitable indicator.*

Teacher's Notes

Teacher Notes

Sample Data

Student data will vary.

Data Table.

Unknown	Potassium Dihydrogen Phosphate	Potassium Hydrogen Sulfate	Potassium Hydrogen Phthalate	Potassium Hydrogen Tartrate
Trial	pH	pH	pH	pH
Sample #1	6.94	2.39	5.26	4.26
Sample #2	6.99	2.32	5.24	4.22

Answers to Post-Lab Questions *(Student answers will vary.)*

1. Average the pH readings for each trial (samples #1 and 2) to calculate the average pK_a value for your unknown weak acid.

   All results have been rounded to one decimal place.

Unknown	Potassium Dihydrogen Phosphate	Potassium Hydrogen Sulfate	Potassium Hydrogen Phthalate	Potassium Hydrogen Tartrate
Average pH (pK_a)	7.0	2.4	5.3	4.2

2. Comment on the precision (reproducibility) of the pK_a determinations. Describe sources of experimental error and their likely effect on the measured pK_a (pH) values.

   The reproducibility of pH measurements is excellent. The pH at the "half-neutralization" point is relatively constant because it depends only on the ratio of the acid and its conjugate base. Small errors in the concentrations of the acid and its conjugate base produce only small changes in this ratio. The observed variation in pH measurements appears to be within the limits of precision of the pH meter. **Note to teacher:** *The pK_a value of an acid depends on temperature. The literature pK_a values are given for a temperature of 25 °C.*

3. The following table lists the identities of the possible unknowns in this experiment. Complete the table by calculating the pK_a value for each acid. *Note:* $pK_a = -\log K_a$.

Acid	Formula	K_a	pK_a
Potassium dihydrogen phosphate	KH_2PO_4	K_{a2} of $H_3PO_4 = 6.2 \times 10^{-8}$	7.2
Potassium hydrogen sulfate	$KHSO_4$	K_{a2} of $H_2SO_4 = 1.2 \times 10^{-2}$	1.9
Potassium hydrogen phthalate	$KHC_8H_4O_4$	K_{a2} of $H_2C_8H_4O_4 = 3.9 \times 10^{-6}$	5.4
Potassium hydrogen tartrate	$KHC_4H_4O_6$	K_{a2} of $H_2C_4H_4O_6 = 4.6 \times 10^{-5}$	4.3

Measuring Acid Strength

Teacher's Notes

4. Compare the pK_a value for your unknown with the information in the table. Determine the probable identity of the unknown.

   The following table compares the experimental and literature values for each unknown. The range of results is sufficient to identify each unknown.

Unknown	KH_2PO_4	$KHSO_4$	$KHC_8H_4O_4$	$KHC_4H_4O_6$
pK_a (Experimental)	7.0	2.4	5.3	4.2
pK_a (Literature)	7.2	2.0	5.4	4.3

5. Write separate equations for the unknown dissolving in water and for the ionization reaction of the weak acid anion that this salt contains.

   Sample equations are shown for potassium dihydrogen phosphate.

   $$KH_2PO_4(s) \longrightarrow K^+(aq) + H_2PO_4^-(aq)$$

   $$H_2PO_4^-(aq) + H_2O(l) \rightleftharpoons HPO_4^{2-}(aq) + H_3O^+(aq)$$

6. Why was it not necessary to know the exact mass of each acid sample?

   It is not necessary to know the exact mass of each acid as long as we know that half of it was neutralized. Since the [HA] and [A⁻] terms cancel out in the equilibrium constant expression, the exact amounts are not important.

7. Why was it not necessary to know the exact concentration of the sodium hydroxide solution?

   Again, the only variable that must be controlled is that half of the acid has been neutralized. It does not matter how much sodium hydroxide is added to neutralize the sample.

8. Why was it necessary to measure the exact volume of distilled water used to dissolve the acid, as well as the exact volume of solution transferred from the beaker to the Erlenmeyer flask?

   The important variable is that half of the acid must be neutralized. Exactly half of the initial volume must be transferred to the Erlenmeyer flask for neutralization. Both the initial volume and transfer volume must therefore be accurately and precisely known.

Teacher Notes

Flinn ChemTopic® Labs — Acids and Bases

Teacher Notes

Classic Titration
pH Curves and an Unknown

Introduction

One of the most common questions chemists have to answer is how much of something is present in a sample or a product. If the product contains an acid or base, these questions are usually answered by titration. Acid–base titrations can be used to measure the concentration of an acid or base in solution and to calculate the formula (molar) mass of an unknown acid or base.

Concepts

- Acids and bases
- Titration
- Neutralization reaction
- Equivalence point
- Titration curve

Background

Titration is a method of *volumetric analysis*—the use of volume measurements to analyze an unknown. In acid–base chemistry, titration is most often used to analyze the amount of acid or base in a sample or solution. Consider a solution containing an unknown amount of hydrochloric acid. In a titration experiment, a known volume of the hydrochloric acid solution would be "titrated" by slowly adding dropwise a *standard* solution of a strong base such as sodium hydroxide. (A standard solution is one whose concentration is accurately known.) The *titrant*, sodium hydroxide in this case, reacts with and consumes the acid via a neutralization reaction *(Equation 1)*. The exact volume of base needed to react completely with the acid is measured. This is called the equivalence point of the titration—the point at which stoichiometric amounts of the acid and base have combined.

$$HCl(aq) + NaOH(aq) \longrightarrow NaCl(aq) + H_2O(l) \qquad \text{Equation 1}$$

Knowing the exact concentration and volume added of the titrant gives the number of moles of sodium hydroxide. The latter, in turn, is related by stoichiometry to the number of moles of hydrochloric acid initially present in the unknown.

Indicators are usually added to acid–base titrations to detect the equivalence point. The endpoint of the titration is the point at which the indicator changes color and signals that the equivalence point has indeed been reached. For example, in the case of the neutralization reaction shown in Equation 1, the pH of the solution would be acidic (< 7) before the equivalence point and basic (> 7) after the equivalence point. The pH at the equivalence point should be exactly 7, corresponding to the neutral products (sodium chloride and water). An indicator that changes color around pH 7 is therefore a suitable indicator for the titration of a strong acid with a strong base.

The progress of an acid–base titration can also be followed by measuring the pH of the solution being analyzed as a function of the volume of titrant added. A plot of the resulting data is called a pH curve or titration curve. Titration curves allow a precise determination of the equivalence point of the titration without the use of an indicator.

The difference between the equivalence point and the endpoint is often poorly understood by students. The equivalence point is a theoretical concept, while the endpoint is what is actually observed in a titration. The indicator endpoint must be selected to be as close as possible to the theoretical equivalence point.

Classic Titration – Page 2

Experiment Overview

The purpose of this experiment is to analyze the shape of the titration curve for neutralization of hydrochloric acid with sodium hydroxide and to determine the concentration of an unknown hydrochloric acid solution. In Part A, pH measurements may be made electronically as a function of time using a pH sensor attached to a computer or calculator-based interface system, or manually as a function of volume added using a pH meter. In Part B, the titration will be repeated with the use of an indicator to detect the endpoint.

Pre-Lab Questions

The approximate concentration of a hydrochloric acid solution is 0.5 M. The exact concentration of this solution is to be determined by titration with 0.215 M sodium hydroxide solution.

1. A 10.00-mL sample of the HCl solution was transferred by pipet to an Erlenmeyer flask and then diluted by adding about 40 mL of distilled water. What is the approximate H_3O^+ concentration and pH of the solution in the flask before the titration begins?

2. Phenolphthalein indicator was added, and the solution in the flask was titrated with 0.215 M NaOH until the indicator just turned pink (pH = 8–9). The exact volume of NaOH required was 22.75 mL. Use the following equation to calculate the concentration of HCl in the original 10.00-mL sample.

$$M_b \times V_b = nM_a \times V_a$$

M_b = molarity of standard base solution M_a = unknown molarity of acid solution
V_b = volume of base added V_a = initial volume of acid solution
n = mole ratio (number of moles of base that react with one mole of acid)

3. One student accidentally "overshot" the endpoint and added 23.90 mL of 0.215 M NaOH. Is the calculated concentration of HCl likely to be too high or too low as a result of this error?

Materials

Hydrochloric acid solution, HCl, unknown concentration, 40 mL
Phenolphthalein indicator solution, 0.5%, 1 mL
Sodium hydroxide (standard) solution, NaOH, approximately 0.1 M, 75 mL*
Water, distilled or deionized
pH Sensor or pH meter
Computer interface system (LabPro)†
Computer or calculator for data collection†
Data collection software (LoggerPro)†
Beakers, 250-mL, 2
Buret, 50-mL
Erlenmeyer flask, 125-mL
Pipet and pipet bulb or filler, 10-mL
Stirrer and stirring bar (optional)
Wash bottle

*Consult your teacher to obtain the precise concentration of sodium hydroxide.
†Optional

Teacher Notes

The accuracy of a titration depends on the accuracy and precision of the glassware used to measure volumes. Discuss with students the design and manufacture of burets and pipets that make them useful for analytical work. It is also very helpful to demonstrate for students the proper technique for rinsing burets and pipets.

Page 3 – **Classic Titration**

Teacher Notes

Safety Precautions

Dilute hydrochloric acid and sodium hydroxide solutions are irritating to skin and eyes. Notify your teacher and clean up all spills immediately with large amounts of water. Phenolphthalein is an alcohol-based solution and is flammable. It is moderately toxic by ingestion. Keep away from flames and other ignition sources. Avoid contact of all chemicals with eyes and skin and wash hands thoroughly with soap and water before leaving the laboratory. Wear chemical splash goggles and chemical-resistant gloves and apron.

Procedure

Part A. Measuring a Titration Curve

1. Using a volumetric pipet, transfer 10.00 mL of the "unknown" hydrochloric acid solution to a 250-mL beaker.

2. Add distilled water to the solution in the beaker until the liquid volume is at about the 50-mL mark.

3. Carefully add a stirring bar to the solution and place the beaker on a magnetic stirrer.

4. Obtain about 75 mL of standard sodium hydroxide solution and record the precise molarity of the solution in Data Table A.

5. Obtain a clean 50-mL buret and rinse it with two 5-mL portions of standard sodium hydroxide solution.

6. Clamp the buret to a ring stand and place a "waste" beaker under the buret. Fill the buret to above the zero mark with sodium hydroxide solution. Open the stopcock to allow any air bubbles to escape from the tip. Close the stopcock when the liquid level in the buret is between the 0- and 10-mL mark.

7. Record the precise level (initial volume) of the solution in the buret. *Note:* Volumes are read from the top down in a buret. Always read from the bottom of the meniscus and remember to include the appropriate number of significant figures. (See Figure 1.)

8. Position the buret over the beaker so that the tip of the buret is within the beaker but at least 2 cm above the liquid surface.

9. If using a pH sensor and computer or calculator-interface system, proceed to step 10. If using a pH meter, proceed to step 22.

Volumetric pipets (A) are more accurate and precise than Mohr or serological pipets (B).

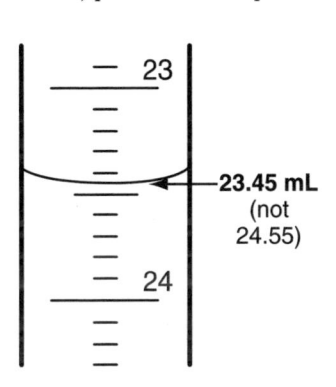

A   B

Figure 1. How to read a buret volume.   **Figure 2.** Setup.

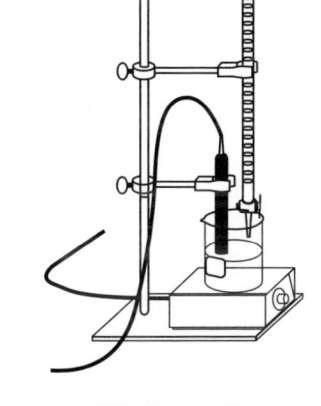

43   Classic Titration

Classic Titration – Page 4

Computer- or calculator-based data collection:

10. Insert a pH sensor into the beaker. Adjust the level of the sensor so that the bottom 2 cm of the sensor is submerged in liquid. Do not allow the sensor to come in contact with the stirring bar. Clamp the sensor in position. (See Figure 2.)

11. Plug the pH sensor into the interface system.

12. Open and format a graph in the data collection software so that the y-axis reads pH on a scale of 0–14.

13. Set the x-axis for time in seconds. Set the minimum and maximum time values at 0 and 300 sec, respectively.

14. Set the time interval to take a reading every second.

15. Wait about 30 seconds to allow the pH sensor to adjust to the solution pH, then press start to begin collecting data.

16. Immediately open the stopcock on the buret and begin adding sodium hydroxide solution slowly to the flask. Adjust the drip rate from the buret to add about one drop per second.

17. Try not to change the drip rate during the course of the titration.

18. The system should automatically record data for the allotted time (300 sec), then stop.

19. Close the stopcock on the buret when data collection has ended. Remove the sensor from the beaker and rinse it with distilled water.

20. Obtain a printout of the titration graph from the computer.

21. *Note:* If proceeding to Part B at this time, save the sodium hydroxide solution in the buret. Skip steps 1–3 in Part B and proceed immediately to step 4.

Alternative procedure using a pH meter:

22. Insert the pH electrode from a pH meter into the beaker. Adjust the level of the electrode so that the bottom 2 cm of the electrode is submerged in liquid. Do not allow the electrode to come in contact with the stir bar. (See Figure 2.)

23. When the pH reading has stabilized, record the initial pH of the solution in Data Table A.

24. Add about 1 mL of sodium hydroxide solution to the beaker. Record the exact buret reading in Data Table A.

25. Record the pH of the solution in Data Table A.

26. Add another 1-mL increment of sodium hydroxide solution. Record both the buret reading and the pH in Data Table A.

27. Continue adding sodium hydroxide in 1-mL portions. Record both the buret reading and the pH after each addition.

28. When the pH begins to increase by more than 0.3 pH units after an addition, decrease the portions of sodium hydroxide added to about 0.2 mL.

29. Continue adding sodium hydroxide in about 0.2 mL increments. Record both the buret reading and the pH after each addition.

Teacher Notes

The alternative procedure may also be used to obtain a computer- or calculator-generated graph of pH versus volume NaOH added. To do this, change the mode setting on the LabPro or CBL-2 interface to "Events with Entry."

Teacher Notes

30. When the pH change is again about 0.3 pH units, resume adding the sodium hydroxide in 1-mL increments. Continue to record both the buret reading and the pH after each addition.

31. Stop the titration when the pH of the solution is greater than 12. Record the final volume of solution in the buret and the final pH.

32. *Note:* If proceeding to Part B at this time, save the sodium hydroxide solution in the buret. Skip steps 1–3 in Part B and proceed immediately to step 4. It may be necessary to refill the buret at this point.

Part B. Analyzing an Unknown

1. Obtain about 75 mL of standard sodium hydroxide solution and record the precise molarity of the solution in Data Table B.

2. Rinse a clean 50-mL buret with two 5-mL portions of the sodium hydroxide solution.

3. Clamp the buret to a ring stand and place a "waste" beaker under the buret. Fill the buret to above the zero mark with sodium hydroxide solution. Open the stopcock to allow any air bubbles to escape from the tip. Close the stopcock when the liquid level in the buret is between the 0- and 10-mL mark.

4. Record the precise level (initial volume) of the solution in the buret in Data Table B. *Note:* Volumes are read from the top down in a buret. Always read from the bottom of the meniscus and remember to include the appropriate number of significant figures. (See Figure 1.)

5. Using a pipet or graduated cylinder, transfer 10.00 mL of the unknown hydrochloric acid solution to a 125-mL Erlenmeyer flask.

6. Add about 20 mL of distilled water to the flask, followed by 2 drops of phenolphthalein indicator.

7. Position the flask under the buret so that the tip of the buret is inside the mouth of the flask. Place a piece of white paper under the flask to make it easier to detect the color change of the indicator at the endpoint.

8. Open the stopcock to allow approximately 5–8 mL of the sodium hydroxide solution to flow into the flask while continuously swirling the flask. Observe the color changes occurring.

9. Continue to add sodium hydroxide slowly, drop-by-drop, while swirling the flask. Use a wash bottle to rinse the sides of the flask with distilled water during the titration.

10. When a faint pink color appears and persists for 10 seconds or more while swirling the flask, the endpoint has been reached. Close the stopcock and record the final buret reading for Trial 1 in Data Table B.

11. Pour the solution out of the flask into the sink and rinse the flask with distilled water.

12. Repeat the titration (steps 4–11) with a second sample of hydrochloric acid. Record all data for Trial 2 in Data Table B.

13. *(Optional)* If time permits, complete a third trial.

Most teachers insist on three trials to obtain precise concentration results. The first trial is generally a survey trial to obtain an estimate of the endpoint volume. The last two trials are then averaged to obtain more precise results.

Classic Titration – *Page 6*

Name: _____

Class/Lab Period: _____

Classic Titration Lab

Data Table A. *Measuring a Titration Curve*

Standard NaOH Concentration			
Initial Buret Reading			
Initial pH			
Buret Reading	**pH**	**Buret Reading (continued)**	**pH**

Data Table B. *Analyzing an Unknown*

Standard NaOH Concentration		
	Initial Buret Reading	**Final Buret Reading**
Trial 1		
Trial 2		
Trial 3 (optional)		

Teacher Notes

Flinn ChemTopic® Labs — Acids and Bases

Teacher Notes

Post-Lab Questions *(Use a separate sheet of paper to answer the following questions.)*

Part A. Measuring a Titration Curve

1. Obtain a graph of the pH curve from Part A. *Note:* If the pH data was collected manually using a pH meter, draw a graph of pH (y-axis) versus volume of NaOH added (x-axis). Label the axes, including the appropriate units.

2. Describe in words how the pH changes during the course of the titration. Be specific.

3. What is the theoretical equivalence point for the titration of a strong acid with a strong base? What happens to the pH of the solution as it approaches the equivalence point?

4. Draw a horizontal line across from the pH at the equivalence point to the titration curve, followed by a vertical line down from this point on the titration curve to the x-axis.

5. Phenolphthalein is often used to detect the endpoint in the titration of a strong acid with a strong base. It changes color from colorless to pink at about pH 9. Draw a horizontal line across from pH 9 to the titration curve, followed by a vertical line down from this point on the titration curve to the x-axis. Is there a large difference between the volume of NaOH added at the equivalence point versus the indicator endpoint? Why or why not?

Part B. Analyzing an Unknown

6. Calculate the unknown molarity of the HCl solution (M_a) for trials 1 and 2, as well as the average molarity. *Note:* See *Prelab Question #2*.

7. Consider the following potential sources of error in the titration. *Fill in the blank:*
   "H" if the error would have caused the calculated molarity of HCl to come out too high.
   "L" if the error would have caused the calculated molarity of HCl to come out too low.
   "N" if the error would have had no effect on the the calculated molarity of HCl.

   a. There was a little distilled water in the Erlenmeyer flask before the titration began. _____

   b. There was a little HCl in the Erlenmeyer flask before the titration began. _____

   c. There was a little distilled water in the buret before you began and you forgot to rinse it out with NaOH. _____

   d. You added 3 drops of phenolphthalein instead of 2 drops. _____

   e. Some NaOH solution dripped into the Erlenmeyer flask before the initial NaOH volume was measured. _____

   f. While you were titrating, some NaOH dripped out onto the table instead of into the Erlenmeyer flask. _____

8. Complete the following sentence with a creative but appropriate analogy: Performing a titration without an indicator is like _____.

Classic Titration

Teacher's Notes
Classic Titration

Master Materials List *(for a class of 30 students working in pairs)*

Hydrochloric acid solution, unknown concentration, 600 mL
Phenolphthalein indicator solution, 0.5%, 25 mL
Sodium hydroxide (standard) solution, NaOH, 0.125 M, 1 L*
Water, distilled or deionized
pH Sensors or pH meters, 15
Computer interface system (LabPro)†
Computer or calculator for data collection†
Data collection software (LoggerPro)†
Beakers, 250-mL, 30
Burets, 50-mL, 15
Erlenmeyer flasks, 125-mL, 15
Pipets and pipet fillers, 10-mL, 15
Magnetic stirrer and stirring bars (optional), 15
Wash bottles, 15

*Remind students to obtain the precise concentration of sodium hydroxide used in this experiment.
†Optional

Preparation of Solutions *(for a class of 30 students working in pairs)*

Hydrochloric Acid, 0.1 M: Add about 500 mL of distilled or deionized water to a flask. Carefully add 8.3 mL of concentrated (12.1 M) hydrochloric acid. Stir to mix, then dilute to 1 L with distilled water.

Phenolphthalein, 0.5%: Add 0.5 g of phenolphthalein to about 50 mL of ethyl alcohol. Mix to dissolve, then dilute to 100 mL with ethyl alcohol.

Sodium Hydroxide, 0.125 M: For best results, prepare the solution fresh before use. Add about 500 mL of distilled water to a flask. Carefully add 5.00 g of sodium hydroxide pellets and stir to dissolve. Dilute to 1 L with distilled water. Use a volumetric flask to obtain precise results.

Safety Precautions

Dilute hydrochloric acid and sodium hydroxide solutions are irritating to skin and eyes. Notify your teacher and clean up all spills immediately with large amounts of water. Phenolphthalein is an alcohol-based solution and is flammable. It is moderately toxic by ingestion. Keep away from flames and other ignition sources. Avoid contact of all chemicals with eyes and skin and wash hands thoroughly with soap and water before leaving the laboratory. Wear chemical splash goggles and chemical-resistant gloves and apron. Please consult current Material Safety Data Sheets for additional safety, handling, and disposal information.

Disposal

Consult your current *Flinn Scientific Catalog/Reference Manual* for general guidelines and specific procedures governing the disposal of laboratory waste. The waste solutions may be flushed down the drain with excess water according to Flinn Suggested Disposal Method #26b.

To encourage student independence, prepare several different "unknown" hydrochloric acid solutions, ranging in concentration from 0.100 to 0.150 M.

Teacher Notes

Lab Hints

- The classic titration lab should be a must-do experiment for every high school student. It teaches students how to use volumetric glassware and encourages them to develop good laboratory technique (especially if they know they will be graded on accuracy). Having students collect pH data and analyze the shape of a titration curve reinforces pH calculations and allows students to "see" what happens in a neutralization reaction.

- Parts A and B of this experiment are independent and may be conducted separately or together. It is not necessary to do Part A in order to complete Part B. If time permits, however, it is recommended that students complete both Parts A and B. The use of technology for data collection and analysis reduces the time needed for Part A to 300 seconds—an excellent use of 5 minutes of lab time!

- Review with students the proper techniques for use of a pipet and buret. The Flinn Scientific Laboratory Techniques Guide (Catalog No. AP6248) contains thumbnail sketches of both, along with 14 other common laboratory techniues.

- At first glance, it might seem that collecting pH data as a function of time rather than volume of titrant would cause the experiment to lose some of its value. A graph of pH versus time over the course of a titration illustrates the initial pH of the acid or base solution, the nature of the equivalence point, the difference between the equivalence point and the indicator endpoint, and the pH of the solution beyond the equivalence point.

Teaching Tips

- Quantitative analysis represents a nearly invisible application of chemistry in our daily lives. To illustrate the hidden importance of quantitative analysis, ask students how they would feel if they could not trust that the water they drink or the medicines they take had been tested to assure their quality and safety.

- The "Microscale Titration" lab in this lab manual provides the perfect opportunity to demonstrate more applications-oriented titrations of vinegar, aspirin, antacids, etc.

- Consider incorporating the titration curve experiment into a collaborative class project comparing and contrasting the titration behavior of strong versus weak acids. Randomly assign student groups one titration curve to perform. Students can then share their data in larger groups to analyze four classic titration curves: (1) strong acid/strong base; (2) weak acid/strong base; (3) strong base/strong acid; and (4) weak base/strong acid. Students should compare the initial pH of the solution, the pH at the equivalence point, and the pH at the midpoint of the titration curve (for weak acids and weak bases, respectively). This is an excellent culminating-type activity to assess student understanding of the principles of acid–base chemistry. See the *Supplementary Information* section for sample graphs of all four types (1–4) of titration curves.

Teacher's Notes

Answers to Pre-Lab Questions *(Student answers will vary.)*

The approximate concentration of a hydrochloric acid solution is 0.5 M. The exact concentration of this solution is to be determined by titration with 0.215 M sodium hydroxide solution.

1. A 10.00-mL sample of the HCl solution was transferred by pipet to an Erlenmeyer flask and then diluted by adding about 40 mL of distilled water. What is the approximate H_3O^+ concentration and pH of the solution in the flask before the titration begins?

   The original HCl solution was diluted about 1 in 5 (10 mL to 50 mL) before titrating. The concentration was therefore reduced by a factor of 5, from 0.5 M to about 0.1 M. The H_3O^+ concentration in a 0.1 M HCl solution is about 0.1 M. The approximate pH of the solution before the titration begins is 1.

   $pH = -log[H_3O^+] = -log(0.1) = 1$

2. Phenolphthalein indicator was added, and the solution in the flask was titrated with 0.215 M NaOH until the indicator just turned pink (pH = 8–9). The exact volume of NaOH required was 22.75 mL. Use the following equation to calculate the concentration of HCl in the original 10.00-mL sample.

   $$M_b \times V_b = nM_a \times V_a$$

   M_b = molarity of standard base solution M_a = unknown molarity of acid solution
   V_b = volume of base added V_a = initial volume of acid solution
   n = mole ratio (number of moles of base that react with one mole of acid)

   n = 1 for titration of hydrochloric acid with sodium hydroxide.

   $$M_a = \frac{(0.215\ M)(22.75\ mL)}{(10.00\ mL)} = 0.489\ M$$

3. One student accidentally "overshot" the endpoint and added 23.90 mL of 0.215 M NaOH. Is the calculated concentration of HCl likely to be too high or too low as a result of this error?

   Overshooting the endpoint will cause the calculated concentration of HCl to be higher than its actual value.

Teacher Notes

Flinn ChemTopic® Labs — Acids and Bases

Teacher Notes

Sample Data

Student data will vary.

Data Table A. *Measuring a Titration Curve*

Standard NaOH Concentration		0.106 M	
Initial Buret Reading		2.20 mL	
Initial pH		1.92	
Buret Reading	pH	Buret Reading (continued)	pH
3.20	2.46	11.50	3.10
4.30	2.49	11.75	3.26
5.55	2.52	11.90	3.44
6.72	2.56	12.20	4.91
7.40	2.58	12.40	8.52
8.50	2.60	12.65	10.32
9.72	2.63	12.90	10.80
10.25	2.67	13.30	10.94
11.30	2.98	13.45	11.13

Data Table B. *Analyzing an Unknown*

Standard NaOH Concentration		0.106 M
	Initial Buret Reading	Final Buret Reading
Trial 1	2.20 mL	12.35 mL
Trial 2	17.40 mL	27.50 mL

Classic Titration

Teacher's Notes

Answers to Post-Lab Questions *(Student answers will vary.)*

Part A. Measuring a Titration Curve

1. Obtain a graph of the pH curve from Part A. *Note:* If the pH data was collected manually using a pH meter, draw a graph of pH (y-axis) versus volume of NaOH added (x-axis). Label the axes, including the appropriate units.

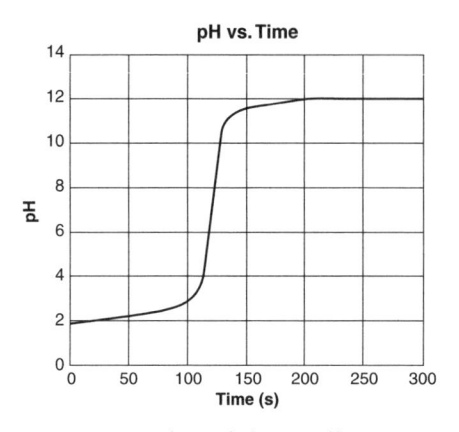

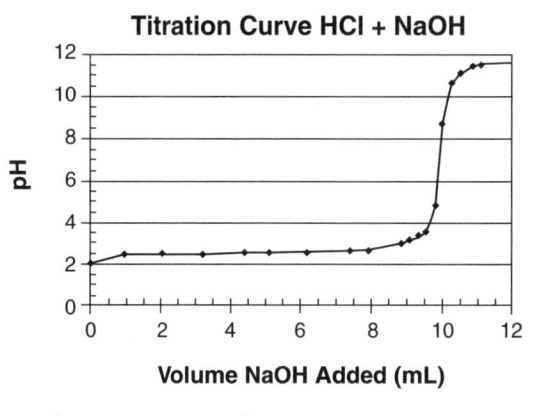

   Computer-based data collection   **Alternative procedure using a pH meter**

2. Describe in words how the pH changes during the course of the titration. Be specific.

   The pH curve is S-shaped. At the beginning of the titration, the pH increases slowly as a function of time (as sodium hydroxide is added). The pH curve is almost horizontal. The pH then begins to increase very rapidly—in fact, the curve of pH versus time (or volume) becomes almost vertical. The pH curve then plateaus out again beyond this region.

3. What is the theoretical equivalence point for the titration of a strong acid with a strong base? What happens to the pH of the solution as it approaches the equivalence point?

   The theoretical equivalence point is pH 7 for neutralization of a strong acid with a strong base (corresponding to a neutral solution). The region approaching the equivalence point corresponds to the steep, almost vertical rise in pH as a function of time (or volume).

4. Draw a horizontal line across from the pH at the equivalence point to the titration curve, followed by a vertical line down from this point on the titration curve to the x-axis.

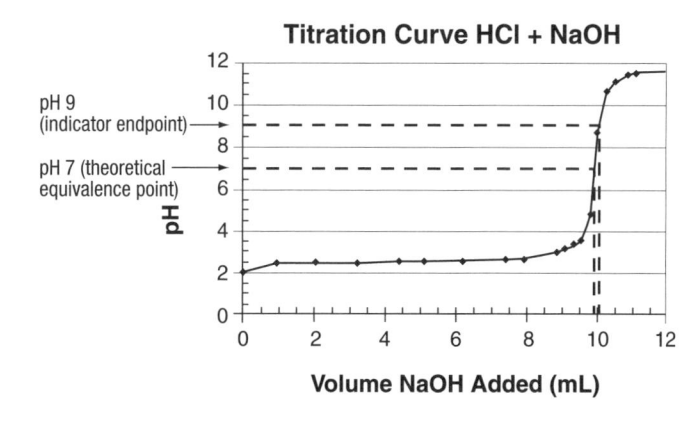

   Lines are shown for both the theoretical equivalence point (Question #4) and the indicator endpoint (Question #5).

Teacher's Notes

Teacher Notes

5. Phenolphthalein is often used to detect the endpoint in the titration of a strong acid with a strong base. It changes color from colorless to pink at about pH 9. Draw a horizontal line across from pH 9 to the titration curve, followed by a vertical line down from this point on the titration curve to the x-axis. Is there a large difference between the volume of NaOH added at the equivalence point versus the indicator endpoint? Why or why not?

   See the sample graph shown on page 52. The difference in NaOH added between pH 7 and pH 9 is less than 0.2 mL. This small difference occurs because the pH rise is very steep in the region around the equivalence point.

Part B. Analyzing an Unknown

6. Calculate the unknown molarity of the HCl solution (M_a) for trials 1 and 2, as well as the average molarity. *Note:* See *Pre-Lab Question #2*.

$$M_b \times V_b = nM_a \times V_a$$

M_b = molarity of standard base solution M_a = unknown molarity of acid solution
V_b = volume of base added V_a = initial volume of acid solution
n = stoichiometric mole ratio (number of moles of base that react with one mole of acid)

   n = 1 for titration of hydrochloric acid with sodium hydroxide.
   Trial 1: M_a = (0.106 M)(10.15 mL)/10.00 mL = 0.108 M
   Trial 2: M_a = (0.106 M)(10.10 ml)/10.00 mL = 0.107 M
   Average molarity = 0.108 M. Excellent precision!

7. Consider the following potential sources of error in the titration. *Fill in the blank:*
   "H" if the error would have caused the calculated molarity of HCl to come out too high.
   "L" if the error would have caused the calculated molarity of HCl to come out too low.
   "N" if the error would have had no effect on the the calculated molarity of HCl.

   a. There was a little distilled water in the Erlenmeyer flask before the titration began. __N__

   b. There was a little HCl in the Erlenmeyer flask before the titration began. __H__

   c. There was a little distilled water in the buret before you began and you forgot to rinse it out with NaOH. __H__

   d. You added 3 drops of phenolphthalein instead of 2 drops. __N__

   e. Some NaOH solution dripped into the Erlenmeyer flask before the initial NaOH volume was measured. __L__

   f. While you were titrating, some NaOH dripped out onto the table instead of into the Erlenmeyer flask. __H__

8. Performing a titration without an indicator is like *dancing without a partner*.
   Encourage creativity!

Classic Titration

Teacher's Notes

Supplementary Information

1. Titration of a strong acid (HCl) with a strong base (NaOH). See the *Sample Data* section.

2. Titration of a weak acid (CH_3COOH) with a strong base (NaOH).

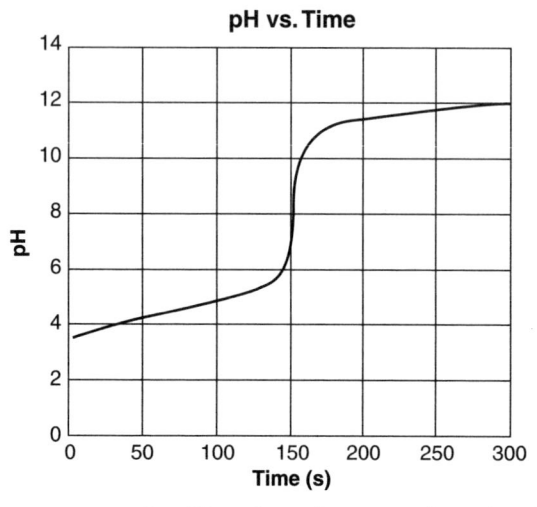

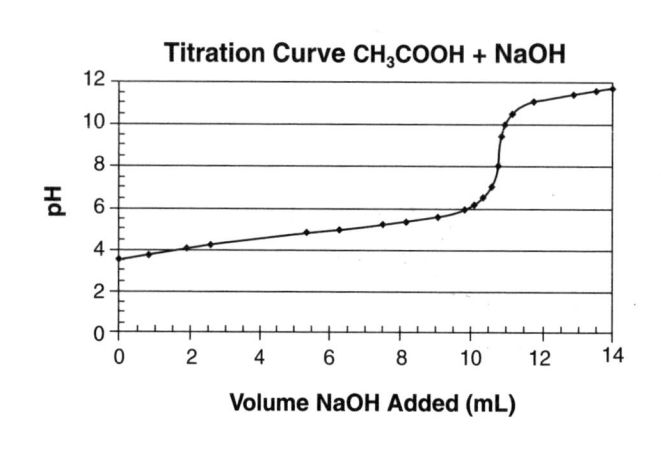

3. Titration of a strong base (NaOH) with a strong acid (HCl).

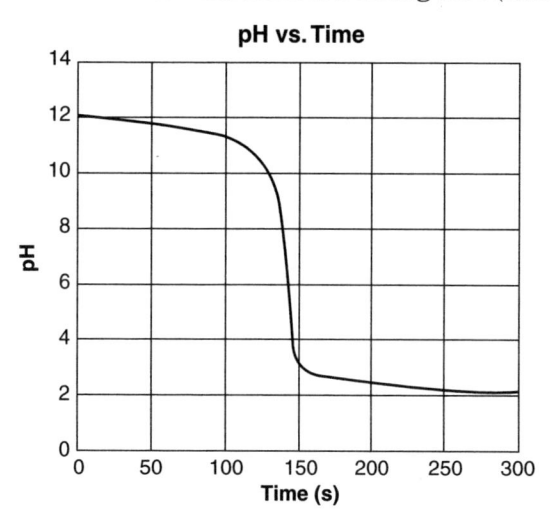

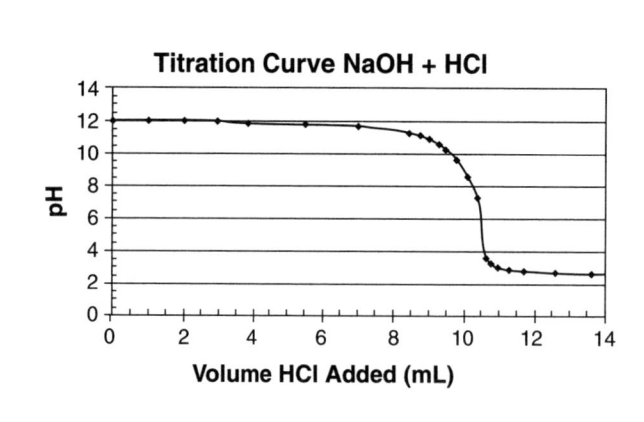

4. Titration of a weak base (NH_3) with a strong acid (HCl).

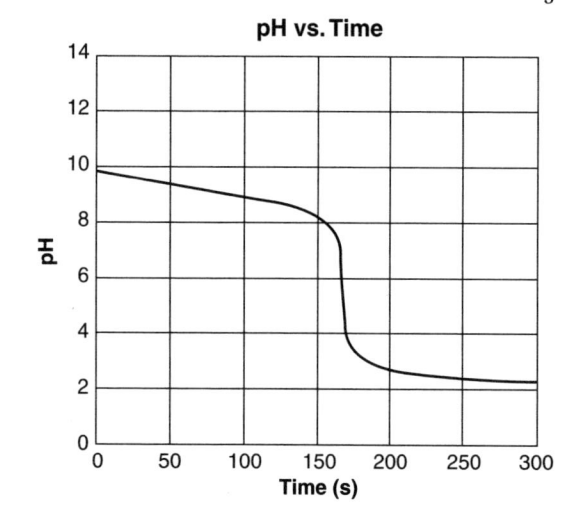

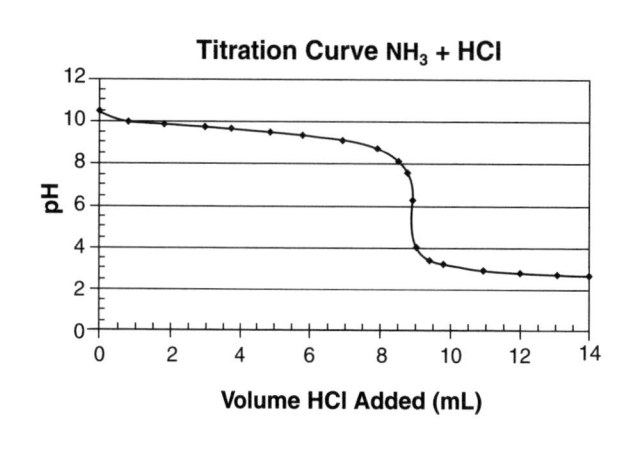

The graphs shown here are actual, not theoretical, graphs obtained by titration of roughly equimolar solutions of acids and bases. Notice the fairly large differences in the pH at the equivalence point, as well as the subtle differences in the shapes of the curves.

Teacher Notes

Microscale Titration
Percent Acetic Acid in Vinegar

Introduction

Vinegar, aspirin, antacids—many common substances that we use every day are acids or bases. The composition or purity of these products is something we normally take for granted. When we take an aspirin tablet, for example, we trust that it does indeed contain the specified amount of aspirin and does not contain unwanted impurities. How can the composition of a commercial product be determined?

Concepts

- Titration
- Neutralization
- Equivalence point
- Molarity

Background

Vinegar is a dilute aqueous solution of acetic acid. It is a natural product that is produced by the fermentation of apple juice (cider vinegar), grapes (wine vinegar), or barley malt (malt vinegar). Federal regulations require that any vinegar sold commercially in the United States contain at least 4% acetic acid by mass. One of the reasons for this requirement is that vinegar is used in the manufacture of pickled and canned foods to prevent the growth of harmful microorganisms. If the amount of acetic acid is less than 4%, the acidity level may not be high enough to prevent the growth of bacteria in the food products.

The amount of acetic acid in vinegar can be determined by microscale titration with a standard solution of sodium hydroxide. Acetic acid, a weak acid, reacts with sodium hydroxide, a strong base, via the neutralization reaction shown in Equation 1.

$$CH_3COOH(aq) + NaOH(aq) \rightarrow NaCH_3COO(aq) + H_2O(l) \qquad \text{Equation 1}$$

In the microscale titration of vinegar, the exact number of drops of sodium hydroxide of known molarity needed to react completely with a measured number of drops of vinegar will be counted. According to Equation 1, one mole of acetic acid reacts exactly with one mole of sodium hydroxide. Another way of saying this is that when all of the acid has been neutralized, the number of moles of acid ($moles_a$) must be equal to the number of moles of base ($moles_b$), as shown in Equation 2.

$$moles_a = moles_b \qquad \text{Equation 2}$$

Molarity is defined as moles of solute per liter of solution (a unit of volume). Rearranging the units in the definition of molarity provides an equation for the number of moles of solute (Equation 3).

$$moles = molarity \times volume = M \times V \qquad \text{Equation 3}$$

Many high school textbooks write the formulas of acetic acid and acetate ion as $HC_2H_3O_2$ and $C_2H_3O_2^-$, respectively. When represented in this way, however, the formulas do not give any intuitive feel for the bonding arrangement of atoms or why one hydrogen is totally different from the others and therefore acidic.

Microscale Titration – Page 2

Combining Equations 2 and 3 gives Equation 4, which can be used to calculate the molarity of acetic acid in vinegar (M_a) based on titration with a standard base solution (M_b).

$$M_a \times V_a = M_b \times V_b \qquad \textit{Equation 4}$$

Notice that volume appears on both sides of Equation 4. Any units of volume, therefore, may be substituted in Equation 4, as long as they are identical for both the acid and base. Thus, volume may be measured in liters, milliliters, or even drops from a pipet, as in the case of microscale titration. Equation 5 will be used to calculate the molar concentration of acetic acid (M_a) in vinegar in this experiment.

$$(M_a)(\text{Drops}_a) = (M_b)(\text{Drops}_b) \qquad \textit{Equation 5}$$

Experiment Overview

The purpose of this experiment is to analyze the percent acetic acid content in vinegar by microscale titration. In Part A, a standard sodium hydroxide solution of known molarity will be prepared. This standard solution will then be used in Part B to titrate vinegar and determine its composition. *Note:* Phenolphthalein is used as an indicator in the titration experiment to detect the endpoint, the point at which the number of moles of acid equals the number of moles of base.

Pre-Lab Questions

The mass–volume percent acetic acid in vinegar is given by the following equation:

$$\% \text{ acetic acid} = \frac{\text{g (acetic acid)}}{\text{mL (vinegar)}} \times 100\% \qquad \textit{Equation 6}$$

A vinegar solution was analyzed by microscale titration and found to be 0.78 M in acetic acid. Carry out the following steps to calculate the percent acetic acid in vinegar.

1. Calculate the molar mass of acetic acid.

2. Use the molar mass of acetic acid and the molarity of the vinegar solution to calculate the number of grams of acetic acid in one liter of vinegar.

3. Use Equation 6 to convert the number of grams of acetic acid in one liter of vinegar to percent. *Note:* Convert one liter to milliliters.

Materials

Phenolphthalein solution, 0.05%, 1 mL
Sodium hydroxide, NaOH, about 0.5 g
Vinegar, about 10 mL
Water, distilled or deionized
Wash bottle
Marker or labeling pen

Balance, centigram (0.01 g precision)
Beakers, 50-mL, 2
Graduated cylinder, 25-mL
Pipets, Beral-type, microtip, 3
Reaction plate, 24-well
White paper (for background)

Teacher Notes

The percent composition of a solution may be stated several different ways. The most common is mass percent, which is equal to grams of solute divided by grams of solution (times 100). Mass percent is equal to mass–volume percent (Equation 6) if the density of the solution is exactly equal to one. This approximation is true (within two significant figures) for vinegar (density = 1.007 g/mL).

Page 3 – Microscale Titration

Teacher Notes

Safety Precautions

Sodium hydroxide is a corrosive solid; it is especially dangerous to the eyes and can cause severe skin burns. Sodium hydroxide solution is also corrosive and toxic. Avoid contact with eyes and skin and notify your teacher immediately in the case of a spill. Phenolphthalein is an alcohol-based solution and is flammable. It is moderately toxic by ingestion. Keep away from flames and other ignition sources. Vinegar is a skin and eye irritant. Wear chemical splash goggles and chemical-resistant gloves and apron. Wash hands thoroughly with soap and water before leaving the laboratory.

Procedure

Part A. Preparing a Standard NaOH Solution

1. Label one 50-mL beaker "B". Measure and record the mass of the beaker in the data table.

2. Add 3–4 sodium hydroxide pellets to the beaker, quickly close the sodium hydroxide container, then reweigh the beaker and pellets and record the combined mass in the data table. *Note:* Work with some haste, since solid sodium hydroxide readily absorbs moisture from the air. This will cause the mass of sodium hydroxide to change.

3. Add 7–8 mL of distilled or deionized water to the beaker. Carefully swirl the mixture to dissolve the pellets. Feel the temperature of the beaker and record whether the solution process is exothermic or endothermic.

4. When the pellets have completely dissolved, pour the solution into a clean 25-mL graduated cylinder.

5. Use a small amount of distilled water (2–3 mL) from a wash bottle to rinse the beaker. Add the rinse solution to the graduated cylinder.

6. Continue rinsing the beaker with small portions of distilled water and pouring the rinse solutions into the graduated cylinder until the total volume in the graduated cylinder is exactly 25.0 mL. Do NOT go above the top line marked on the graduated cylinder!

7. Dry the original 50-mL beaker and pour the sodium hydroxide solution back into this beaker labeled "B". *Note:* "B" is for base.

Part B. Titrating Commercial Vinegar Solutions

8. Obtain a 24-well reaction plate and place it on top of a piece of white paper.

9. Label a second 50-mL beaker "V" and obtain about 10 mL of vinegar in the beaker. Record the brand of vinegar used in the data table.

10. Label two microtip pipets "B" and "V" and place them in their respective beakers.

11. Using pipet V, add 15 drops of white vinegar into well A1. *Note:* For best results, hold the pipet in a nearly vertical position. This will help ensure equal-sized drops.

Remind students that the calculations used in this experiment (Equation 5) will be accurate only if the size of the drops is reproducible. It is therefore important that students develop good technique in delivering equal-sized drops.

Microscale Titration

Microscale Titration – Page 4

Teacher Notes

12. Using a clean pipet, add 1 drop of phenolphthalein indicator to the vinegar.

13. Using pipet B, slowly add the sodium hydroxide solution one drop at a time to the vinegar sample in well A1.

14. Count the exact number of drops of sodium hydroxide required to give the solution a faint red color that does not fade with mixing and that lasts at least 20 seconds. Record the number of drops of NaOH in the data table.

15. Repeat steps 11–14 four more times using separate wells on the reaction plate. Record the results for each trial in the data table.

16. Drain the microtip pipets and discard them in the trash.

17. Rinse the beakers and the microscale reaction plate thoroughly with water.

Teacher Notes

Name: _____

Class/Lab Period: _____

Microscale Titration

Data Table

Part A. Preparing a Standard NaOH Solution

Mass of empty beaker (g)	
Mass of beaker + NaOH (g)	
Volume of water (mL)	
Exothermic or endothermic?	

Part B. Titrating Commercial Vinegar Solutions

Brand of Vinegar	
Titration Trial	Number of drops of NaOH added
1	
2	
3	
4	
5	

Post-Lab Questions *(Use a separate sheet of paper to answer the following questions.)*

1. Calculate the mass of sodium hydroxide used and the molarity of the standard sodium hydroxide solution prepared in Part A.

2. Use Equation 5 (see the *Background* section) to calculate the molarity of the vinegar solution for each trial 1–5.

3. Calculate the average molarity of the vinegar solution. Use the range of molarity values calculated for Trials 1–5 to estimate a "plus-or-minus" error for the average molarity (e.g., 0.78 ±0.05 M)

4. Follow the steps outlined in the *PreLab Questions* to convert the average molarity of the vinegar solution to the percent of acetic acid in vinegar. *Note:* Consider the appropriate number of significant figures to include in the result.

5. Refer to the *Background* section: Based on your results, is the vinegar that you tested "legal"?

6. Step 7 in Part A specifies that the beaker used to store the freshly made sodium hydroxide solution should be completely dry. Why is this important?

7. Explain why the procedure described in Part B could not be used to analyze "red wine vinegar". How could the procedure be modified to analyze this type of vinegar?

Microscale Titration

Teacher's Notes
Microscale Titration

Master Materials List *(for a class of 30 students working in pairs)*

Phenolphthalein solution, 0.05%, 25 mL
Sodium hydroxide, NaOH, 10 g
Vinegar, 150 mL
Water, distilled or deionized
Wash bottles, 15
Markers or labeling pens, 15
Balances, centigram (0.01 g precision), 3
Beakers, 50-mL, 30
Graduated cylinders, 25-mL, 15
Pipets, Beral-type, microtip, 45
Reaction plates, 24-well, 15
White paper (for background)

Preparation of Solutions *(for a class of 30 students working in pairs)*

Phenolphthalein Solution, 0.05%: Dissolve 0.05 g phenolphthalein in 50 mL of 95% ethyl alcohol. Stir to dissolve and dilute to 100 mL with ethyl alcohol.

Sodium Hydroxide, 0.40 M (optional): Add 4.00 g of sodium hydroxide pellets to 100 mL of distilled or deionized water in a flask. Stir to dissolve and allow the exothermic solution to cool to room temperature. Dilute to 250 mL with distilled water. *Note:* This solution is needed only if students will not be preparing their own standard sodium hydroxide solutions in Part A.

Safety Precautions

Sodium hydroxide is a corrosive solid; it is especially dangerous to the eyes and can cause severe skin burns. Sodium hydroxide releases a great deal of heat when it dissolves in water; the resulting solution is corrosive and toxic. Avoid contact with eyes and skin and notify your teacher immediately in the case of a spill. Keep citric acid on hand to use in case of sodium hydroxide spills. Phenolphthalein is an alcohol-based solution and is flammable. It is moderately toxic by ingestion. Keep away from flames and other ignition sources. Wear chemical splash goggles and chemical-resistant gloves and apron. Wash hands thoroughly with soap and water before leaving the laboratory. Please consult current Material Safety Data Sheets for additional safety, handling, and disposal information.

Disposal

Consult your current *Flinn Scientific Catalog/Reference Manual* for general guidelines and specific procedures governing the disposal of laboratory waste. The waste solutions may be flushed down the drain with excess water according to Flinn Suggested Disposal Method #26b.

Lab Hints

- Microscale titration represents a convenient alternative to traditional titration experiments using burets and pipets. We recommend the "Classic Titration" experiment in this Flinn ChemTopic Labs™ manual to illustrate the use of volumetric glassware and to teach students the importance of good laboratory technique. Once students have completed a classic titration, however, microscale titration provides a fast and effective way to apply the principles of titration to the analysis of consumer products.

The phenolphthalein solution used in this experiment is especially dilute. This helps ensure more accurate results in microscale titrations where the quantities are so small. It also avoids permanent staining of the microscale reaction plates. The 0.05% phenolphthalein solution may be conveniently prepared by 1:10 dilution of commercially available 0.5% solution.

Teacher's Notes

Teacher Notes

- The advantages of microscale titration are that the amount of chemicals and the time needed for preparation are greatly reduced, disposal problems are minimized, and the procedure itself is fast and easy to perform. Students can repeat the titration several times, which improves both the accuracy and precision of the analysis. Both parts of this experiment can easily be completed within one 50-minute lab period.

- It is not necessary to do Part A in order to complete Part B. The molarity of the sodium hydroxide solution prepared in Part A will be about 0.4 M. This concentration can be prepared with reliable precision using centigram (0.01-g) balances and 25-mL graduated cylinders. If fewer than three balances are available for a class of 30 students working in pairs, there will be an inevitable bottleneck at the balance station for Part A. In this case, consider substituting a ready-made sodium hydroxide solution of known molarity for use by students in Part B. See the *Preparation of Solutions* section for instructions on how to prepare 0.40 M sodium hydroxide for student use.

- The most important variable that affects the reliability of microscale titration experiments is the reproducibility of the drop size delivered to the reaction wells. Reproducible drop volumes are easily achieved using the special microtip pipets (Flinn Catalog No. AP1517) described in the *Materials* section. The best way to deliver same-size drops is to hold the pipet vertically above the reaction well. With such small volumes being used, it is also critical to expel any air bubbles in the pipet before counting drops.

- If microtip pipets are not available, they may be prepared by "drawing out" standard thin stem pipets (Flinn Catalog No. AP1444). Hold the bulb of a thin stem pipet in one hand, with the thumb and index finger positioned at the point where you wish the drawn out portion of the stem to begin. With the free hand, wrap the exposed portion of the stem around the index finger. Gently stretch the stem to lengthen it to about 3 inches, then cut the drawn-out stem to desired length.

- Having students determine the average volume of a drop of liquid is a valuable optional exercise. To do this, fill a 10-mL graduated cylinder to the 1.00-mL mark, then add water dropwise. Measure and record the volume of water in the graduated cylinder after 10, 20, 30, and 40 drops of water have been added. Average the volume of 10 drops of water and then divide by 10 to calculate the average volume of one drop. This exercise may help students develop good lab technique so that the size of a single drop is more reproducible and precise.

- More accurate results may be obtained by carrying out the titration by mass instead of by volume—that is, by measuring the mass of sodium hydroxide needed to titrate a known mass of vinegar. This can be done by weighing the appropriate microtip pipets before and after the solutions have been dispensed. To obtain reliable mass measurements, increase the number of drops of vinegar to 25–30 drops.

Teaching Tips

- Two separate biochemical processes, both of which require microorganisms, are involved in the production of vinegar. In the first stage, natural sugars in fruits and grains are converted to alcohol by the action of *Saccharomyces* yeast (Step 1). This is an anaerobic process—it occurs in the absence of oxygen. The second stage involves further oxidation

Sodium hydroxide solution may be standardized by titration with potassium hydrogen phthalate (KHP). Reagent-grade KHP is considered a "primary standard."

Microscale Titration

Teacher's Notes

of alcohol to acetic acid by *Acetobacter* bacteria (Step 2). This is an aerobic process and thus requires exposure to oxygen in air.

$$C_6H_{12}O_6 \rightarrow 2CH_3CH_2OH + 2CO_2 \qquad \text{Step 1}$$
$$\text{sugar} \qquad \text{alcohol}$$

$$CH_3CH_2OH + O_2 \rightarrow CH_3COOH + H_2O \qquad \text{Step 2}$$
$$\text{alcohol} \qquad \text{acetic acid}$$

- Microscale titration provides an excellent method for the analysis of a wide variety of consumer products that contain acids and bases. See the *Supplementary Information* section for a sample procedure and results for the analysis of aspirin. Other products that may be analyzed include antacids and fruit juices.

- "Upset Tummy? MOM to the Rescue!" in the *Demonstrations* section of this Flinn ChemTopic™ Labs manual illustrates the titration of milk of magnesia, a popular antacid. The demonstration uses hydrochloric acid and universal indicator to simulate the process that occurs in the stomach as antacids neutralize excess stomach acid.

- It may be interesting for students to compare the acidity in different types of vinegar. European vinegars, in particular, tend to run a bit stronger than American brands and some Mediterranean vinegars may contain as much as 8–9% acetic acid.

Answers to Pre-Lab Questions *(Student answers will vary.)*

The mass–volume percent acetic acid in vinegar is given by the following equation:

$$\% \text{ acetic acid} = \frac{g \text{ (acetic acid)}}{mL \text{ (vinegar)}} \times 100\% \qquad \text{Equation 6}$$

A vinegar solution was analyzed by microscale titration and found to be 0.78 M in acetic acid. Carry out the following steps to calculate the percent acetic acid in vinegar.

1. Calculate the molar mass of acetic acid.

   Molar mass ($C_2H_4O_2$) = (2 × 12.01) + (4 × 1.008) + (2 × 16.00) = 60.05 g/mole

2. Use the molar mass and the molarity of the vinegar solution to calculate the mass in grams of acetic acid in one liter of vinegar.

   $$\text{Mass (acetic acid)} = \frac{0.78 \text{ moles}}{1 \text{ L vinegar}} \times \frac{60 \text{ grams}}{1 \text{ mole}} = 47 \text{ grams/L}$$

3. Use Equation 6 to convert the number of grams of acetic acid in one liter of vinegar to percent. *Note:* Convert one liter to milliliters.

   $$\text{Percent acetic acid in vinegar} = \frac{47 \text{ g}}{L} \times \frac{1 \text{ L}}{1000 \text{ mL}} \times 100\% = 4.7\%$$

Teacher's Notes

Teacher Notes

Sample Data

Student data will vary.

Data Table

Part A. Preparing a Standard NaOH Solution	
Mass of empty beaker (g)	26.30
Mass of beaker + NaOH (g)	26.75
Volume of water (mL)	25.0
Exothermic or endothermic?	Exothermic

Part B. Titrating Commercial Vinegar Solutions	
Brand of Vinegar	Store brand white cider vinegar
Titration Trial	Number of drops of NaOH added
1	27 drops
2	30 drops
3	26 drops
4	29 drops
5	29 drops

Answers to Post-Lab Questions *(Student answers will vary.)*

1. Calculate the mass of sodium hydroxide used and the molarity of the standard sodium hydroxide solution prepared in Part A.

   Mass of NaOH used = 26.75 g − 26.30 g = 0.45 g

   $$\frac{0.45 \text{ g NaOH}}{25.0 \text{ mL}} \times \frac{1 \text{ mole}}{40.0 \text{ g}} \times \frac{1000 \text{ mL}}{1 \text{ L}} = 0.45 \text{ M}$$

2. Use Equation 5 (see the *Background* section) to calculate the molarity of the vinegar solution for each trial 1–5.

   $$M_a = \frac{M_b \times V_b}{V_a}$$

   Note to teacher: $M_b = 0.45$ *M and* $V_a = 15$ *drops in each trial.*
   Trial 1: $M_a = (0.45 \text{ M})(27 \text{ drops})/(15 \text{ drops}) = 0.81 \text{ M}$
   Trial 2: $M_a = (0.45 \text{ M})(30 \text{ drops})/(15 \text{ drops}) = 0.90 \text{ M}$
   Trial 3: $M_a = (0.45 \text{ M})(26 \text{ drops})/(15 \text{ drops}) = 0.78 \text{ M}$
   Trial 4: $M_a = (0.45 \text{ M})(29 \text{ drops})/(15 \text{ drops}) = 0.87 \text{ M}$
   Trial 5: $M_a = (0.45 \text{ M})(29 \text{ drops})/(15 \text{ drops}) = 0.87 \text{ M}$

Teacher's Notes

3. Calculate the average molarity of the vinegar solution. Use the range of molarity values calculated for Trials 1–5 to estimate a "plus-or-minus" error for the average molarity (e.g., 0.78 ±0.03 M).

$$\text{Average molarity} = \frac{(0.84\ M + 0.90\ M + 0.78\ M + 0.87\ M + 0.87\ M)}{5} = 0.85\ M$$

Molarity range (Trials 1–5) = 0.78–0.90 M
Estimated error in molarity = 0.85 ±0.05 M

Note to teacher: *This is an estimate! The error in the average is normally reported as the average deviation (sum of the differences between each individual result and the average, divided by the number of results).*

4. Follow the steps outlined in the *Pre-Lab Questions* to convert the average molarity of the vinegar solution to the percent of acetic acid in vinegar. *Note:* Consider the appropriate number of significant figures to include in the result.

$$\text{Mass (acetic acid)} = \frac{0.85\ \text{moles}}{1\ L\ \text{vinegar}} \times \frac{60\ \text{grams}}{1\ \text{mole}} = 51\ \text{grams/L}$$

$$\text{Percent acetic acid in vinegar} = \frac{51\ g}{L} \times \frac{1\ L}{1000\ mL} \times 100\% = 5.1\%$$

5. Refer to the *Background* section: Based on your results, is the vinegar that you tested "legal"?

    Yes, the percent acetic acid is above the 4% minimum required by law.

6. Step 7 in Part A specifies that the beaker used to store the freshly made sodium hydroxide solution should be completely dry. Why is this important?

    If the beaker contains residual water, it will dilute the sodium hydroxide concentration. Because the solution is more dilute, more would have to be added to neutralize the vinegar. The calculated molarity of the vinegar would be too high as a result.

7. Explain why the procedure described in Part B could not be used to analyze "red wine vinegar." How could the procedure be modified to analyze this type of vinegar?

    The color of the red wine vinegar would mask the color of the phenolphthalein endpoint. The procedure could be modified to provide a different means of detecting the endpoint. This could be done by measuring the actual pH at the equivalence point or using a different indicator that would provide a more visible color change at a pH of about 9.

Teacher's Notes

Teacher Notes

Supplementary Information

Microscale Titration of Aspirin

Aspirin is acetylsalicylic acid, a monoprotic weak acid. When aspirin is dissolved in water, it ionizes to give its conjugate base and H_3O^+ ions, according to Equation 1.

$$\text{C}_6\text{H}_4(\text{OCOCH}_3)\text{CO}_2\text{H} + H_2O \rightleftharpoons \text{C}_6\text{H}_4(\text{OCOCH}_3)\text{CO}_2^- + H_3O^+ \quad \text{Equation 1}$$

A regular-strength aspirin tablet usually contains 325 mg of acetylsalicylic acid per tablet. The amount of acetylsalicylic acid is easily analyzed using microscale titration to determine the composition and purity of an aspirin tablet.

Acetylsalicylic acid is not very soluble in water. To prepare a solution for analysis, grind one regular-strength aspirin tablet in a mortar and pestle and dissolve the powder in about 10 mL of ethyl alcohol. Add enough distilled water to the aspirin/alcohol mixture to make 500 mL of solution. There will be some insoluble residue (starch and binder) present. This residue should not interfere with the titration.

Sample Titration Procedure

1. Place a 24-well reaction plate on top of a piece of white paper.

2. Using a microtip pipet, add 25 drops of aspirin solution to well A1, followed by 1 drop of 0.05% phenolphthalein indicator solution. For best results, do NOT add more than one drop of indicator.

3. Titrate the aspirin solution in well A1 dropwise with 0.010 M sodium hydroxide solution from a microtip pipet.

4. Count the number of drops of sodium hydroxide required to reach a pink or red-violet endpoint.

5. Repeat steps 2–4 five more times and record the number of drops of sodium hydroxide required for each trial.

6. Calculate the average number of drops of sodium hydroxide for trials 1–6.

Sample Data Table

Titration Trial	1	2	3	4	5	6	Avg.
Drops of NaOH	9	9	10	10	9	9	9

For best results, use only regular, noncoated aspirin tablets. Coated aspirin tablets contain ingredients that may interfere with the titration.

Microscale Titration

Teacher's Notes

Sample Calculations

Molarity (acetylsalicylic acid) = $\dfrac{(0.010 \text{ M NaOH}) \times (9 \text{ drops NaOH})}{25 \text{ drops aspirin}}$ = 0.0036 M

Molecular formula (acetylsalicylic acid) = $C_9H_8O_4$

Molar mass (acetylsalicylic acid) = (9 × 12.01) + (8 × 1.008) + (4 × 16.00) = 180.2 g/mole

Mass of acetylsalicylic acid per tablet = $\dfrac{0.0036 \text{ moles}}{1 \text{ L}} \times \dfrac{180.2 \text{ g}}{\text{mole}} \times 0.5 \text{ L}$ = 0.32 g

Note: The last factor (0.5 L) in the above equation represents the fact that the original aspirin tablet was dissolved in 500 mL (not 1 L) of solution.

Purity of aspirin tablet = (320 mg/325 mg) × 100% = 98%

Teacher Notes

Buffers Keep the Balance
Biological Buffers

Introduction

A buffer protects against rapid changes in pH when acids or bases are added to it. Every living cell contains natural buffer systems to maintain the constant pH needed for proper cell function. Consumer products are also often buffered to safeguard their activity. What are buffers made of? How do buffers maintain the delicate pH balance needed for life and health?

Concepts

- pH
- Buffer
- Conjugate base
- Weak acid

Background

Many chemical reactions in living organisms take place at neutral pH values. Even a small change in pH can cause some of nature's catalysts (the enzymes) to stop functioning. The pH level in blood, for example, must be maintained within extremely narrow limits.

The ability of buffers to resist changes in pH upon addition of acid or base can be traced to their chemical composition. All buffers contain a mixture of either a weak acid (HA) and its conjugate base (A^-), or a weak base and its conjugate acid. The buffer components HA and A^- are related to each other by means of the following chemical reaction that describes the behavior of a weak acid in water (Equation 1).

$$\underset{\text{weak acid}}{HA} + H_2O \rightleftharpoons \underset{\text{conjugate base}}{A^-} + H_3O^+ \qquad \textit{Equation 1}$$

Buffers control pH because the two buffer components are able to react with and therefore neutralize either strong acid or strong base that might be added to the solution. The weak acid component HA reacts with any strong base, such as sodium hydroxide (NaOH), to give water and the conjugate base component A^- (Equation 2). The conjugate base component A^- reacts with any strong acid, such as hydrochloric acid (HCl), to give its acid partner HA and chloride ion (Equation 3).

$$HA + NaOH \rightleftharpoons Na^+ + A^- + H_2O \qquad \textit{Equation 2}$$

$$A^- + HCl \rightleftharpoons HA + Cl^- \qquad \textit{Equation 3}$$

These neutralization reactions can be visualized as a cyclic process (Figure 1). Buffer activity will continue as long as both components are present in solution. Once either component is consumed, the buffer capacity will be exhausted and the buffer will no longer be effective.

A buffer composed of an equal number of moles of a weak acid and its conjugate base is called an *ideal buffer* because it is equally effective in resisting pH changes upon addition of either acid or base. The pH range in which a buffer system will be effective is called its *buffer range*. The

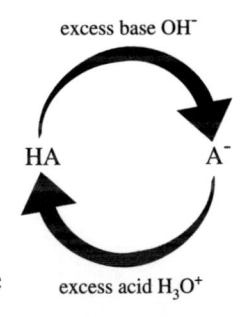

Figure 1.

Buffers are considered an advanced topic in the acid–base curriculum, and many teachers may neglect the topic for this reason. This is unfortunate, since buffers integrate many of the core principles in acid–base chemistry and also have many applications in biology, ecology, and consumer products. These applications are often very interesting to students.

Buffers Keep the Balance – Page 2

buffer range is usually limited to 2 pH units centered around the pH of the ideal buffer solution. An ideal carbonic acid–bicarbonate buffer, for example, has a pH of 6.4 and its buffer range is pH 5.4–7.4.

Properties of Biological Buffers

The body is able maintain proper pH due to the presence of chemical buffer systems in cells and in the blood. The major buffer present in blood, for example, is composed of the weak acid, carbonic acid (H_2CO_3), and its conjugate base, bicarbonate ion (HCO_3^-) (Equation 4). The normal pH of blood (7.2) is at the upper limit of the effective range for the carbonic acid–bicarbonate buffer system. The buffer activity is kept in balance, however, by a reserve supply of gaseous CO_2 in the lungs, which can replenish H_2CO_3 in the blood by dissolving and reacting with water in the blood (Equation 5).

$$H_2CO_3 + H_2O \rightleftharpoons HCO_3^- + H_3O^+ \qquad \textit{Equation 4}$$

$$\underset{\text{lungs}}{CO_2(g)} \rightleftharpoons \underset{\text{blood}}{CO_2(aq)} + H_2O \rightleftharpoons H_2CO_3 \qquad \textit{Equation 5}$$

The second most important biological buffer involves dihydrogen phosphate ($H_2PO_4^-$) as the weak acid and its conjugate base hydrogen phosphate (HPO_4^{2-}) (Equation 6). An ideal buffer composed of equal moles of $H_2PO_4^-$ and HPO_4^{2-} has a pH range of 6.8–7.2. This is an optimum value for physiological pH. An ideal phosphate buffer is the most prominent buffer within cells.

$$H_2PO_4^- + H_2O \rightleftharpoons HPO_4^{2-} + H_3O^+ \qquad \textit{Equation 6}$$

Experiment Overview

In Part A, seltzer water is used as a source of carbonic acid to prepare a model biological carbonic acid–bicarbonate buffer. The effects of added acid and base on the pH and the buffer capacity of this model buffer will be examined. The pH value of the buffer solution will be estimated using bromthymol blue, an acid–base indicator that changes color in the pH range 6.0 to 7.6. Bromthymol blue is yellow when the pH is less than 6.0, blue when the pH is greater than 7.6, and green (the intermediate color) in the transition range 6.0–7.6.

In Part B, two different phosphate buffers will be prepared. These buffers reflect the physiological role of buffers within cells. The pH of the buffers and the pH range over which they are effective will be measured. The pH changes will be followed using universal indicator, an acid–base indicator that can be used over the pH 4–10 range. Consult the universal indicator color chart to determine the pH value corresponding to a given color of the solution.

Teacher Notes

As noted in the overview, the emphasis in this lab is on qualitative properties of buffers. Calculations are kept to a minimum in order to focus on what a buffer is made of and how it works.

Page 3 – **Buffers Keep the Balance**

Teacher Notes

Pre-Lab Questions

1. a) Using Equation 1 as a guide, write an equation for the reaction of acetic acid (CH₃COO**H**) with water.

   b) Identify the conjugate base of acetic acid in the reaction equation.

   Hint: The **H** atom highlighted in boldface is the acidic or "active" hydrogen in acetic acid.

2. Acetic acid and a salt containing its conjugate base, such as sodium acetate, form buffer solutions that are effective in the pH range 3.7–5.7.

   a) What would be the composition and pH of an ideal buffer prepared from acetic acid and its salt, sodium acetate?

   b) In resisting a pH change, which buffer component would react with NaOH?

   c) What happens to the buffer activity when this component is exhausted?

Materials

Bromthymol blue indicator solution, 0.04%, 3 mL
Hydrochloric acid, HCl, 0.1 M, 8 mL
Seltzer water, H₂CO₃, 8 mL
Sodium bicarbonate solution, NaHCO₃, 0.1 M, 8 mL
Sodium hydroxide solution, NaOH, 0.1 M, 8 mL
Sodium phosphate (monobasic) solution, NaH₂PO₄, 0.1 M, 20 mL
Sodium phosphate (dibasic) solution, Na₂HPO₄, 0.1 M, 12 mL
Universal indicator, 5 mL
Beakers, 50-mL, 2
Beral-type pipets, graduated, 7
Distilled or deionized water
Graduated cylinders, 10-mL, 2
pH paper, narrow range, 6.0–8.0
Reaction plate, 24-well
Stirring rod
Test tubes (medium), 6
Test-tube rack
Universal indicator color chart

Safety Precautions

Dilute solutions of sodium bicarbonate, hydrochloric acid, and sodium hydroxide are body tissue irritants. Avoid exposure to eyes and skin. Wear chemical splash goggles and chemical-resistant gloves and apron.

Buffers Keep the Balance

Buffers Keep the Balance – Page 4

Procedure

Part A. Model Carbonate Blood Buffer

1. Set up six medium-size test tubes in a rack. Label them 1–6.

2. With Table 1 as a guide, use a graduated cylinder to measure and add the indicated volumes of the required solutions to each test tube.

3. Mix the contents of each test tube thoroughly by gentle shaking or swirling.

Table 1.

Test Tube Number	1	2	3	4	5	6
Solution	Carbonic Acid (Reference)	Model Carbonate Blood Buffer	Water (Control)	Model Carbonate Blood Buffer	Water (Control)	Sodium Bicarbonate (Reference)
Seltzer water (mL)	4	2	0	2	0	0
Sodium bicarbonate (mL)	0	2	0	2	0	4
Distilled water (mL)	0	0	4	0	4	0

4. Add 5 drops of bromthymol blue to each test tube 1–6. Shake to mix. Record the initial color of each solution 1–6 in Data Table A.

5. Measure the initial pH of each solution using a piece of narrow-range pH paper, pH 6.0–8.0. Record the results in Data Table A.

6. Using a Beral-type pipet, add 0.1 M hydrochloric acid solution *dropwise* to the model carbonate blood buffer in test tube 2. Be sure to swirl the contents after each drop to ensure thorough mixing.

7. *Count the number of drops* of HCl required to change the color to the same shade as the carbonic acid reference solution in test tube 1. Record the number of drops in Data Table A.

8. Using a Beral-type pipet, add 0.1 M hydrochloric acid solution *dropwise* to the water (control) in test tube 3. *Count the number of drops* of HCl required to change the color to the same shade as the carbonic acid reference solution in test tube 1. Record the number of drops in Data Table A.

9. Using a different Beral-type pipet, add 0.1 M sodium hydroxide solution *dropwise* to the model carbonate blood buffer in test tube 4. Be sure to swirl the contents after each drop to ensure thorough mixing.

10. *Count the number of drops* of NaOH required to change the color to the same shade as the sodium bicarbonate reference solution in test tube 6. Record the number of drops in Data Table A.

Teacher Notes

Flinn ChemTopic™ Labs — Acids and Bases

11. Using a Beral-type pipet, add 0.1 M sodium hydroxide solution *dropwise* to the water (control) in test tube 5. *Count the number of drops* of NaOH required to change the color to the same shade as the sodium bicarbonate reference solution in test tube 6. Record the number of drops in Data Table A.

Part B. Biological Phosphate Buffers

12. Obtain two 50-mL beakers and label them A and B.

13. Use clean graduated cylinders to add 12 mL of NaH_2PO_4 solution and 3 mL of Na_2HPO_4 solution to beaker A. (This is **Buffer A**.)

14. Use clean graduated cylinders to add 8 mL of NaH_2PO_4 solution and 8 mL of Na_2HPO_4 solution to beaker B. (This is **Buffer B**.)

15. Stir each buffer solution with a stirring rod to ensure thorough mixing.

16. Use the following layout plan to fill each indicated well in a 24-well reaction plate with 1.5 mL of distilled water (the control), Buffer A, or Buffer B, respectively.

17. Add 3 drops of universal indicator to each filled well.

18. Record the initial indicator colors for the water control (well A1), Buffer A (well A2) and Buffer B (well A3) in Data Table B.

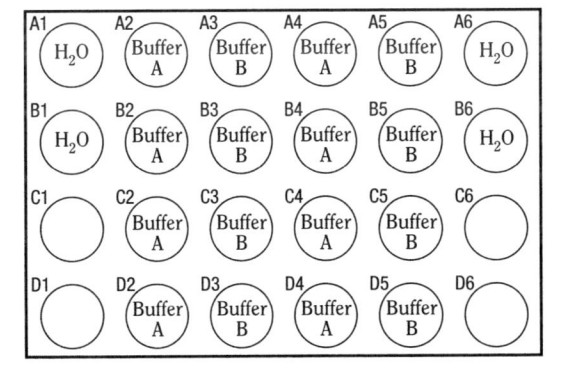

19. Estimate the initial pH of wells A1, A2, and A3 using narrow-range (6.0–8.0) pH paper.

Effect of HCl Addition:

20. Using a clean Beral-type pipet, add 1 drop of HCl to wells B1, B2, and B3. Record the indicator colors in Data Table B.

21. Add 5 drops of HCl to wells C2 and C3 and record the new indicator colors in Data Table B.

22. Add 10 drops of HCl to wells D2 and D3 and again record the indicator colors in Data Table B.

Effect of NaOH Addition:

23. Using a clean Beral-type pipet, add 1 drop of NaOH to wells B4, B5, and B6. Record the indicator colors in Data Table C.

24. Add 5 drops of NaOH to wells C4 and C5 and record the indicator colors in Data Table C.

25. Add 10 drops of NaOH to wells D4 and D5 and again record the indicator colors in Data Table C.

26. Wash the contents of the reaction well plate down the drain under running water.

Name: _____

Class/Lab Period: _____

Buffers Keep the Balance

Data Table A. *Model Carbonate Blood Buffer*

Test Tube Number	1	2	3	4	5	6
Solution	Carbonic Acid (Reference)	Model Carbonate Blood Buffer	Water (Control)	Model Carbonate Blood Buffer	Water (Control)	Sodium Bicarbonate (Reference)
Bromthymol blue indicator color						
Initial pH value						
Number of drops of HCl required to convert solutions 2 and 3 to acid reference color	NA			NA	NA	NA
Number of drops of NaOH required to convert solutions 4 and 5 to bicarbonate reference color	NA	NA	NA			NA

Data Table B. *Effect of HCl on Biological Phosphate Buffers*

	Estimated pH (pH paper)	Universal Indicator Color			
		Initial	After 1 drop of HCl	After 5 drops of HCl	After 10 drops of HCl
Water (control)				NA	NA
Buffer A					
Buffer B					

Page 7 – Buffers Keep the Balance

Teacher Notes

Data Table C. *Effect of NaOH on Biological Phosphate Buffers*

	Estimated pH (pH paper)	Universal Indicator Color			
		Initial	After 1 drop of NaOH	After 5 drops of NaOH	After 10 drops of NaOH
Water (control)				NA	NA
Buffer A					
Buffer B					

Post-Lab Questions *(Use a separate sheet of paper to answer the following questions.)*

1. Compare the measured pH value for the model carbonate blood buffer to (a) the expected pH of an ideal carbonic acid–bicarbonate buffer, and (b) the actual pH of blood.

2. Based on the pH comparisons in Question #1, which solution, the model carbonate blood buffer or an actual blood buffer, is more likely to contain a greater proportion of the carbonic acid component compared to the bicarbonate component? Explain.

3. What is the effect of adding even 1 drop of HCl or NaOH on the pH value of the control (water)? Compare this to the effect of adding HCl or NaOH to the model carbonate blood buffer.

4. Which phosphate buffer in Part B corresponds to the composition of an ideal buffer solution? Compare its measured pH value with the calculated pH of the ideal buffer.

5. Use the universal indicator color chart to compare the observed pH changes for phosphate buffers A and B and the control (water) upon addition of HCl and NaOH. Were phosphate buffers A and B equally effective in resisting pH changes upon addition of either HCl or NaOH?

Teachers who have covered equilibrium constant calculations with their classes may choose to add a question relating the pH of an ideal buffer to the K_a value of the weak acid.

$$\frac{[A^-][H_3O^+]}{[HA]} = K_a$$

In an ideal buffer, $[A^-] = [HA]$ and $[H_3O^+] = K_a$. Taking the negative logarithm of both sides reveals that the pH of an ideal buffer is equal to the pK_a of the weak acid component.

Teacher's Notes
Buffers Keep the Balance

Master Materials List *(for a class of 30 students working in pairs)*

    Bromthymol blue solution, 0.04%, 75 mL
    Hydrochloric acid, HCl, 0.1 M, 150 mL
    Seltzer water, H_2CO_3, 8-oz bottle (240 mL)
    Sodium bicarbonate solution, $NaHCO_3$, 0.1 M, 150 mL
    Sodium hydroxide solution, NaOH, 0.1 M, 150 mL
    Sodium phosphate (monobasic) solution, NaH_2PO_4, 0.1 M, 350 mL
    Sodium phosphate (dibasic) solution, Na_2HPO_4, 0.1 M, 225 mL
    Universal indicator, 100 mL
    Beakers, 50-mL, 30
    Beral-type pipets, graduated, 105
    pH paper, narrow range, 6.0–8.0, 1 roll
    Distilled or deionized water
    Graduated cylinders, 10-mL, 30
    Reaction plates, 24-well, 15
    Stirring rods, 15
    Test-tube racks, 15
    Test tubes, 16 × 150 mm, 90
    Universal indicator overhead color chart (optional)

Preparation of Solutions

Bromthymol Blue, 0.04%: Dissolve 0.04 g of bromthymol blue in 50 mL of distilled or deionized water. Mix to dissolve, then dilute to 100 mL with distilled water.

Hydrochloric Acid, 0.1 M: Add about 100 mL of distilled or deionized water to a flask. Carefully add 2.1 mL of concentrated hydrochloric acid (12.1 M). Stir to mix, then dilute to 250 mL with distilled water.

Sodium Bicarbonate, 0.1 M: Dissolve 2.1 g of sodium bicarbonate in 100 mL of distilled or deionized water. Mix to dissolve, then dilute to 250 mL with distilled water.

Sodium Hydroxide, 0.1 M: Add about 100 mL of distilled or deionized water to a flask. Carefully add 1.0 g of sodium hydroxide pellets and stir to dissolve. Dilute to 250 mL with distilled water.

Sodium Phosphate (Monobasic), 0.1 M: Dissolve 6.9 g of sodium phosphate monobasic monohydrate ($NaH_2PO_4 \cdot H_2O$) in 200 mL of distilled or deionized water. Mix to dissolve, then dilute to 500 mL with distilled water.

Sodium Phosphate (Dibasic), 0.1 M: Dissolve 13.4 g of sodium phosphate dibasic heptahydrate ($Na_2HPO_4 \cdot 7H_2O$) in 200 mL of distilled or deionized water. Mix to dissolve, then dilute to 500 mL with distilled water.

Index-card sized color charts are attached to every bottle of universal indicator sold by Flinn Scientific. A large transparency of the color chart suitable for overhead projector use is also available.

Teacher Notes

Teacher's Notes

Safety Precautions

Dilute solutions of sodium bicarbonate, hydrochloric acid and sodium hydroxide are body tissue irritants. Avoid exposure to eyes and skin. Wear chemical splash goggles and chemical-resistant gloves and apron. Consult current Material Safety Data Sheets for additional safety, handling, and disposal information.

Disposal

Consult your current *Flinn Scientific Catalog/Reference Manual* for general guidelines and specific procedures governing the disposal of laboratory waste. All solutions can be disposed of according to Flinn Scientific Disposal Method # 26b.

Lab Hints

- The experimental work for this lab can reasonably be completed in one 50-minute lab period. The Pre-Lab questions should be completed prior to lab.

- Flinn pH meters (Catalog No. AP8673) provide an inexpensive and convenient way to measure pH values of solutions directly on a microscale reaction plate. Consider adding the more precise measurement of pH using a pH meter as a valuable extension of the procedures in Parts A and B.

Answers to Pre-Lab Questions *(Student answers will vary.)*

1. a) Using Equation 1 as a guide, write an equation for the reaction of acetic acid (CH_3COOH) with water.

   b) Identify the conjugate base of acetic acid in the reaction equation.

   a) $CH_3COOH + H_2O \rightleftharpoons CH_3COO^- + H_3O^+$

   b) The conjugate base of acetic acid has the formula CH_3COO^-; it is called acetate ion.

2. Acetic acid and a salt containing its conjugate base, such as sodium acetate, form buffer solutions that are effective in the pH range 3.7–5.7.

   a) What would be the composition and pH of an ideal buffer prepared from acetic acid and its conjugate base, sodium acetate?

   b) In resisting a pH change, which buffer component would react with NaOH?

   c) What happens to the buffer activity when this component is exhausted?

   a) An ideal buffer contains equal numbers of molecules of both the weak acid and its conjugate base component. The pH of the ideal buffer is the middle value in the pH range of a given buffer system. An ideal acetic acid–sodium acetate buffer solution, therefore, would have a pH value of 4.7.

   b) When NaOH, a strong base, is added to a buffer solution, it reacts with and is neutralized by the weak acid component of the buffer, in this case, acetic acid.

   c) If sufficient strong base is added to the buffer to consume completely the weak acid component, then the buffer will no longer be effective. Any additional acid or base added to the solution would then cause a large change in pH.

Teacher's Notes

Sample Data

Student data will vary

Data Table A. Model Carbonate Blood Buffer

Test Tube Number	1	2	3	4	5	6
Solution	Carbonic Acid (Reference)	Model Carbonate Blood Buffer	Water (Control)	Model Carbonate Blood Buffer	Water (Control)	Sodium Bicarbonate (Reference)
Bromthymol blue indicator color	yellow	green	teal green	green	teal green	blue
Initial pH value	< 6.0	6.8–7.0	7.0–7.2	6.8–7.0	7.0–7.2	> 8.0
Number of drops of HCl required to convert solutions 2 and 3 to acid reference color	NA	35–40 drops	1 drop	NA	NA	NA
Number of drops of NaOH required to convert solutions 4 and 5 to bicarbonate reference color	NA	NA	NA	20–25 drops	1 drop	NA

Data Table B. Effect of HCl on Biological Phosphate Buffers

	Estimated pH (pH paper)	Universal Indicator Color			
		Initial	After 1 drop of HCl	After 5 drops of HCl	After 10 drops of HCl
Water (control)	7.0	teal green	red	NA	NA
Buffer A	6.0	yellow-gold	yellow-gold	orange	red
Buffer B	6.8	light green	light green	yellow-green	yellow

Teacher's Notes

Teacher Notes

Data Table C. *Effect of NaOH on Biological Phosphate Buffers*

	Estimated pH (pH paper)	Universal Indicator Color			
		Initial	After 1 drop of NaOH	After 5 drops of NaOH	After 10 drops of NaOH
Water (control)	7.0	teal green	purple	NA	NA
Buffer A	6.0	yellow-gold	yellow-gold	yellow-green	light green
Buffer B	6.8	light green	light green	green	dark green

Answers to Post-Lab Questions *(Student answers will vary.)*

1. Compare the measured pH value for the model carbonate blood buffer to: (a) the expected pH of an ideal carbonic acid–bicarbonate buffer, and (b) the actual pH of blood.

    The model carbonate blood buffer prepared in Part A has a pH value equal to 6.8–7.0. This is greater than the pH of an ideal carbonic acid–bicarbonate buffer (6.4). The pH of the model blood buffer is lower, however, than the actual pH of blood, which is regulated at pH = 7.2 ±0.2.

2. Based on the pH comparisons in Question #1, which solution, the model carbonate blood buffer or an actual blood buffer, is more likely to contain a greater proportion of the carbonic acid component compared to the bicarbonate component? Explain.

    The pH of the model carbonate blood buffer indicates that it is more acidic than the actual buffer present in blood. Therefore, it is more likely that the model buffer contains a greater amount of the weak acid component relative to the bicarbonate (conjugate base) component.

3. What is the effect of adding even 1 drop of HCl or NaOH on the pH value of the control (water)? Compare this to the effect of adding HCl or NaOH to the model carbonate blood buffer.

    The pH of water was dramatically affected by the addition of even one drop of strong acid or strong base. For example, addition of 1 drop of HCl was sufficient to decrease the pH to the "acid" color (pH <6). In contrast, the buffer solution was approximately 35 times more resistant to pH change, since 35–40 drops of HCl were necessary to change the pH of the buffer solution to the acid color. The model carbonate blood buffer was not quite as resistant to the effect of NaOH as it was to the effect of HCl. The buffer capacity with respect to NaOH addition, however, was still 15–20 times greater than that of water.

Buffers Keep the Balance

Teacher's Notes

4. Which phosphate buffer in Part B corresponds to the composition of an ideal buffer solution? Compare its measured pH value with the calculated pH of the ideal buffer.

   Phosphate buffer B, containing equal amounts of the weak acid component (NaH$_2$PO$_4$) and its conjugate base (Na$_2$HPO$_4$), has the composition of an ideal buffer. Its measured pH (6.8) is slightly lower than the calculated pH (7.0) of the ideal phosphate buffer.

5. Use the universal indicator color chart to compare the observed pH changes for phosphate buffers A and B and the control (water) upon addition of HCl and NaOH. Were phosphate buffers A and B equally effective in resisting pH changes upon addition of either HCl or NaOH?

   Buffers A and B were both more resistant than the water control to pH change. The pH of water dropped from 7 (teal) to < 4 (red) upon addition of 1 drop of HCl. Addition of 1 drop of NaOH to water caused an equally steep pH change in the opposite direction, from pH 7 (teal) to > 11 (purple). The ideal phosphate buffer was able to stay within a narrow pH range from 6.0 to 8.0 (yellow to dark green) upon addition of 10 drops of either HCl or NaOH. Buffer A was also able to resist change upon addition of NaOH. It was not as effective, however, when HCl was added to the solution.

Demonstrations

Teacher Notes

Indicator Sponge
A Discrepant Event Demonstration

Introduction

The discrepant event of placing a red sponge in a red solution and having it turn blue is sure to capture your students' attention and stimulate a lively discussion of possible explanations.

Concepts

- Acids and bases
- Indicators

Materials

Congo red indicator, 1 g

Hydrochloric acid, HCl, 1 M, 100 mL

Sodium hydroxide, NaOH, 1 M, 100 mL

Red food coloring, 1 mL

Blue food coloring, 1 mL

Beakers or large jars, 1000-mL or larger, 2

Tongs (optional)

Sponge

Gloves

Safety Precautions

Hydrochloric acid is corrosive to skin and eyes and toxic by ingestion and inhalation. Sodium hydroxide solution is corrosive to skin and eyes. Wear chemical splash goggles, chemical-resistant gloves, and a chemical-resistant apron. Please consult current Material Safety Data Sheets for additional safety information.

Indicator Preparation

Make a 1% solution of Congo red indicator by adding 1 g of Congo red to 100 mL of distilled or deionized water. Rinse the sponge (including new sponges) with water to remove residual soap, surfactants, or acids. If the sponge is too large for the beaker of indicator solution, cut the sponge in half. Place the sponge in the Congo red solution, immersing it completely. Wearing rubber gloves to keep from staining hands, periodically squeeze out the liquid. Allow the sponge to soak in the liquid for about 15 minutes. Squeeze out as much liquid as possible and rinse the sponge with fresh water a few times. The indicator sponge is now ready to use. The remaining Congo red solution can be used to make additional indicator sponges.

Preparation for Demonstration

1. Add 100 mL of 1 M hydrochloric acid to a 1000- or 2000-mL beaker. Fill the beaker about 3/4 full with tap water.

2. Add enough red food coloring (about 1 mL per 1000 mL solution) to the acid solution in the beaker until it is a deep red color.

3. Add 100 mL of 1 M sodium hydroxide solution to a 1000- or 2000-mL beaker. Fill the beaker about 3/4 full with tap water.

4. Add enough blue food coloring to the basic solution in the beaker until it is a deep blue color.

5. If the sponge is red, wet the sponge with tap water and rinse it out.

6. If the sponge is blue, place the sponge in the base solution to convert it to a red color.

"Indicator Sponge" is available as a Chemical Demonstration Kit from Flinn Scientific (Catalog No. AP6160).

Demonstrations

Procedure

Teacher Notes

1. Slowly place the red sponge into the beaker containing the red acid solution. Use tongs or a gloved hand. The sponge will immediately turn blue!

2. Remove the sponge and squeeze out as much red acid solution as possible back into the acid beaker.

3. *(Optional)* Rinse the sponge in tap water to show that the sponge is actually blue and is not just saturated with a blue solution. This step minimizes the amount of acid and base being transferred between solutions.

4. Slowly place the blue sponge into the beaker containing the blue base solution. Use tongs or a gloved hand. The sponge will immediately turn red!

5. Remove the sponge and squeeze out as much blue base solution as possible back into the blue beaker.

6. Rinse the sponge in tap water, if necessary, to show that the sponge is actually red and is not just saturated with a red solution.

7. Repeat the demonstration as desired. The sponge may be reused indefinitely.

Disposal

The acid and base solutions may be used several times before they become neutralized or the dyes start to decompose. When ready to dispose, simply mix the two solutions to neutralize them and then pour down the sink with excess water according to Flinn Suggested Disposal Method #26b. Please consult your current *Flinn Scientific Catalog/Reference Manual* for proper disposal procedures.

Tips

- Food coloring will stain fingers and clothing—wear gloves and an apron. Light-colored, cellulose sponges work best in this application.

- The concentration of the acid and base solutions is not critical as long as they are above 0.05 M. If the sponge is rinsed out between the acid and base treatment, then the two solutions do not even have to be the same concentration.

- Rinsing the sponge out between each color change will keep the acid and base solutions fresher. It minimizes the amount of acid and base and also the amount of food coloring transferred between beakers. *Note:* The liquid coming out of the sponge is the color of the solution and not the color of the sponge.

Discussion

Congo red is a dye, a biological stain, and a pH indicator. It has been used as a direct fabric dye for cotton to produce a bright red fabric. Biologists use Congo red as a general contrast stain for cellulose. The color transition is between pH 3.0 and 5.0. Below a pH of 3.0, the indicator is blue. Above pH 5.0, the indicator is red.

When the cellulose sponge is soaked in a Congo red solution, the dye becomes permanently bonded to the cellulose fibers. The active acid/base sites on Congo red are still available and the sponge now becomes an indicator sponge for acids. It can also be used to check for acid spills on counters after students have worked in the lab.

Use the indicator sponge as a safety demonstration after students have worked with acids and bases in the lab. Wipe the sponge over the surface of the lab benches to check for spills.

Flinn ChemTopic® Labs — Acids and Bases

Demonstrations

Teacher Notes

The Rainbow Tube
Chemical Demonstration

Introduction

Saturated sodium carbonate solution is added to a test tube containing a dilute solution of hydrochloric acid and universal indicator. A rainbow column of colors develops in the tube as the dense sodium carbonate solution sinks to the bottom and carbonate ions gradually diffuse upward and neutralize the hydrochloric acid solution.

Concepts

- Acids and bases
- Indicators
- pH
- Neutralization

Materials

Hydrochloric acid, HCl, 0.1 M, 20 mL

Sodium carbonate solution, Na_2CO_3, saturated, 6 mL

Universal indicator, 3 mL

Pipets, Beral-type, 2

Test tube, large, 20 × 150 mm

Test tube rack

Safety Precautions

Dilute hydrochloric acid and saturated sodium carbonate solutions are skin and eye irritants. Avoid contact of all chemicals with eyes and skin. Universal indicator is an alcohol-based solution and is flammable. Keep away from flames and other ignition sources. Wear chemical splash goggles and chemical-resistant gloves and apron. Please consult current Material Safety Data Sheets for additional safety, handling, and disposal information.

Procedure

1. Add about 3 mL of universal indicator, followed by 20 mL of hydrochloric acid solution, to a large test tube. Swirl the test tube to mix.

2. Fill a Beral-type pipet with saturated sodium carbonate solution.

3. Tilt the test tube slightly and slowly squeeze the saturated sodium carbonate solution down the side of the test tube. Do not attempt to layer the solutions. The sodium carbonate solution will sink to the bottom of the test tube.

4. Refill the Beral-type pipet with a second portion of saturated sodium carbonate and add it to the test tube as well.

5. Hold the test tube vertically and set it in a test tube rack. Colored layers form immediately as carbonate ions diffuse upward and react with hydrogen ions in the acidic solution.

Prepare saturated sodium carbonate solution by adding 25 g of sodium carbonate to 100 mL of distilled water. Stir to dissolve. After one hour, decant off the solution.

The Rainbow Tube

Demonstrations

Teacher Notes

6. Observe the gradual appearance of a rainbow spectrum of colored layers in the tube. Relate the colors to the reactions taking place in the test tube and the resulting pH changes.

Disposal

The rainbow tube contents may be washed down the drain with plenty of excess water according to Flinn Suggested Disposal Method #26b. Please consult your current *Flinn Scientific Catalog/Reference Manual* for general guidelines and specific procedures governing the disposal of laboratory waste.

Tips

- The rainbow column of colors will last for a week or more if the test tube is left undisturbed.

- Colored layers develop in the test tube in the following order, from top to bottom: red, orange, yellow, green, blue, and purple. Discuss the order of colors within the test tube and their significance.

Discussion

The initial hydrochloric acid solution has a pH of about 1 and turns red in the presence of universal indicator. Saturated sodium carbonate contains more than 20 grams of solute per 100 mL of solution and has a density of 1.1–1.2 g/mL. Because the sodium carbonate solution has a greater density than the hydrochloric acid–universal indicator mixture, the sodium carbonate solution immediately settles to the bottom of the test tube. The sodium carbonate solution has a pH of about 12 and turns purple in contact with universal indicator.

Carbonate and sodium ions diffuse upward through the solution to balance the concentration gradient in the test tube. In the process, a neutralization reaction takes place between carbonate ions and hydrogen ions in solution and different colored layers develop at various depths in the test tube. The colors of the layers reflect different hydrogen ion concentrations as the diffusion and neutralization processes balance each other out.

The balanced net ionic equations for the neutralization reactions between sodium carbonate and hydrochloric acid are as follows:

$$H^+(aq) + CO_3^{2-}(aq) \rightarrow HCO_3^-(aq)$$

$$H^+(aq) + HCO_3^-(aq) \rightarrow H_2CO_3(aq)$$

$$H_2CO_3(aq) \rightarrow H_2O(l) + CO_2(g)$$

Flinn ChemTopic® Labs — Acids and Bases

Demonstrations

Teacher Notes

Upset Tummy? MOM to the Rescue!
Colorful Antacid Demonstration

Introduction

Mix milk of magnesia (MOM) with universal indicator and observe the dramatic spectrum of color changes as the antacid dissolves in simulated stomach acid! This is a great demonstration to illustrate acid–base neutralization, solubility, and "antacid-testing" consumer chemistry.

Concepts

- Acid–base neutralization
- Solubility
- Antacids

Materials

Milk of magnesia, 20 mL
Hydrochloric acid, HCl, 3 M, ~ 20 mL
Universal indicator, 4–5 mL
Water, distilled or deionized, 800 mL
Beaker, 1-L (or other large beaker)

Beral-type pipets, 2
Graduated cylinder, 25-mL or 50-mL
Ice, crushed (or ice cubes)
Magnetic stir plate (or stirring rod)
Magnetic stir bar

Safety Precautions

Milk of magnesia is intended for laboratory use only; it has been stored with other non–food-grade laboratory chemicals and is not meant for human consumption. Hydrochloric acid solution is toxic by ingestion and inhalation and is corrosive to skin and eyes. Universal indicator solution is an alcohol-based flammable solution. Consult current Material Safety Data Sheets for further safety and handling techniques. Wear chemical splash goggles, chemical-resistant gloves, and a chemical-resistant apron.

Procedure

1. Measure 20 mL of milk of magnesia using a graduated cylinder and pour it into a 1-L beaker.

2. Place the 1-L beaker on a magnetic stir plate. Add a magnetic stir bar to the beaker.

3. Add water and crushed ice (or ice cubes) to give a total volume of approximately 750 mL. Turn on the stir plate so as to create a vortex in the mixture.

4. Add about 5 mL (2-pipets full) of universal indicator solution. Watch as the white suspension of milk of magnesia turns to a deep purple color. The color indicates that the solution is basic.

5. Add 2–3 mL (1-pipet full) of 3 M HCl. The mixture quickly turns red and then goes through the entire range of universal indicator color changes back to purple.

6. Repeat this process, adding HCl one-pipet full at a time, waiting after each addition until the mixture turns back to blue–purple.

"Upset Tummy? MOM to the Rescue!" is available as a Chemical Demonstration Kit from Flinn Scientific (Catalog No. AP5934).

Demonstrations

7. The process can be repeated a number of times before all of the Mg(OH)$_2$ dissolves and reacts with the HCl. As more acid is added, the color changes begin to occur more slowly and eventually the suspension completely dissolves. The final solution will be clear and red.

Disposal

Neutralize the final solution according to Flinn Suggested Disposal Method #24b. Excess milk of magnesia can be disposed of according to Flinn Suggested Disposal Method #26a. Please consult your current *Flinn Scientific Catalog/Reference Manual* for proper disposal procedures.

Tips

- The recommended acid concentration in this demonstration is 3 M, in order to allow the reaction to go to completion with a reasonable volume of acid.

- Adding ice to the demonstration slows down the reaction and results in longer-lasting colors. As the ice melts, the color changes speed up.

Discussion

The active ingredient in milk of magnesia is magnesium hydroxide, Mg(OH)$_2$. Magnesium hydroxide forms a suspension in water since it has a very low solubility—0.0009 g/100 mL in cold water and 0.004 g/100 mL in hot water.

Initially in the demonstration, the solution is basic due to the small amount of Mg(OH)$_2$ that goes into solution. Universal indicator gives the mixture a violet color, indicating a pH of about 10. (See Universal Indicator Color Chart below.) Upon addition of hydrochloric acid (the simulated "stomach acid"), the mixture quickly turns red as the acid disperses throughout the beaker and neutralizes the small amount of dissolved Mg(OH)$_2$. A small amount of excess acid is present and solution is acidic (pH < 4).

			Universal Indicator Color Chart				
Color	Red	Orange	Yellow	Green	Green–blue	Blue	Violet
pH	4	5	6	7	8	9	10

Excess acid, however, causes more Mg(OH)$_2$ from the suspension to dissolve. As more of the Mg(OH)$_2$ goes into solution, it neutralizes the excess acid, and the solution reverts back to its purple, basic color. The addition of universal indicator allows this entire sequence to be observed. During the process, the color of the mixture cycles through the entire universal indicator color range—from red to orange to yellow to green to blue and finally back to violet. By adding more "stomach acid," the process can be repeated many times before all of the Mg(OH)$_2$ dissolves and is neutralized. The final solution, after all the Mg(OH)$_2$ has dissolved and reacted with HCl, is clear and red.

Teacher Notes

The effect of acid on the solubility of magnesium hydroxide may be viewed as an application of equilibrium and LeChâtelier's Principle.

$$Mg(OH)_2(s) \rightleftarrows Mg^{2+}(aq) + 2OH^-(aq)$$

Excess H$^+$ reacts with and removes OH$^-$ from solution, which shifts the above equilibrium to the right—more Mg(OH)$_2$ dissolves.

Flinn ChemTopic® Labs — Acids and Bases

Teacher Notes

Strong vs. Weak Acids
Chemical Demonstration

Introduction

Not all acids are created equal. This demonstration compares the "frothing and foaming" activity of different acids with calcium carbonate and examines their behavior in the presence of their conjugate bases to define strong versus weak acids. The use of a "rainbow acid" universal indicator produces a rainbow spectrum of color changes as the mixtures react.

Concepts

- Strong acid
- Conjugate base
- Weak acid
- pH

Materials

Acetic acid, CH_3COOH, 1 M, 400 mL
Calcium carbonate, $CaCO_3$, 40 g
Hydrochloric acid, HCl, 1 M, 400 mL
Sodium acetate, $NaCH_3CO_2$, 16 g
Sodium chloride, NaCl, 12 g

Demonstration tray, large
Hydrometer cylinders, 600-mL, 4
Graduated cylinder, 250-mL
"Rainbow acid" universal indicator, 5 mL
Water, distilled or deionized

Safety Precautions

Hydrochloric acid and acetic acid solutions are toxic and corrosive. Avoid contact with skin and eyes. "Rainbow acid" universal indicator solution is an alcohol-based solution and is flammable. Avoid contact with flames or other ignition sources. Wear chemical splash goggles, chemical-resistant gloves, and a chemical-resistant apron. Please consult current Material Safety Data Sheets for additional safety information.

Procedure

1. Obtain 4 large hydrometer cylinders or tall-form beakers and place them on a large demonstration tray. Label the cylinders #1–4.

2. Using a graduated cylinder, add 200 mL of 1 M hydrochloric acid to cylinders #1 and 2.

3. Using a graduated cylinder, add 200 mL of 1 M acetic acid to cylinders #3 and 4.

4. Add about 1 mL of "rainbow acid" universal indicator to cylinders #1 and 3. Compare the color and pH of hydrochloric acid versus acetic acid.

5. Write equations for the ion-forming reactions of hydrochloric acid and acetic acid in water. Identify the "common ion" (conjugate base) of each.

6. Add 12 g of sodium chloride, followed by about 1 mL of "rainbow acid" universal indicator, to cylinder #2. Mix to dissolve. Compare the color and pH of solutions #1 and 2.

7. Add 16 g of sodium acetate, followed by about 1 mL of "rainbow acid" universal indicator, to cylinder #4. Mix thoroughly to dissolve. Compare the color and pH of solutions #3 and 4. What effect does adding acetate ion have on the pH of acetic acid?

Demonstrations

8. Add 10 g of calcium carbonate to each cylinder #1–4.

9. Compare the amount of frothing and foaming in each cylinder. Relate the activity of the solutions to pH, the difference between strong and weak acids, and the "common ion" effect.

Disposal

Waste solutions may be disposed down the drain with excess water according to Flinn Suggested Disposal Method #26b. Please consult your current *Flinn Scientific Catalog/Reference Manual* for general guidelines and specific procedures governing the disposal of laboratory waste.

Tips

- To save time, pre-measure the amounts of solids needed for the demonstration.

- The use of a demonstration tray to catch any spillover is strongly recommended—a solid wall of foam may erupt out of the hydrometer cylinders.

- "Rainbow acid" universal indicator (Flinn Catalog No. U0012) contains a combination of indicators and produces a rainbow spectrum of colors for acid solutions having pH values between 1 and 7. Use the accompanying color chart to estimate the pH of acids.

Discussion

Hydrochloric acid and acetic acid ionize in water to produce hydrogen ions (H_3O^+) and their conjugate bases, chloride ion and acetate ion, respectively (Equations 1 and 2).

$$HCl(aq) + H_2O(l) \rightarrow H_3O^+(aq) + Cl^-(aq) \qquad \text{Equation 1}$$

$$CH_3COOH(aq) + H_2O(l) \rightarrow H_3O^+(aq) + CH_3COO^-(aq) \qquad \text{Equation 2}$$

Comparing the pH of these two acid solutions indicates that more H_3O^+ ions are produced in HCl than in CH_3COOH. All of the HCl molecules undergo ionization to form H_3O^+ ions. Most of the CH_3COOH molecules, however, are not ionized and only a few H_3O^+ ions are produced.

Reaction with calcium carbonate reinforces the pH comparison. The rate of reaction of $CaCO_3$ with an acid depends on the concentration of H_3O^+ ions in solution (Equation 3). The rate of reaction and amount of foaming (CO_2 evolution) are greater for HCl than CH_3COOH, suggesting again that the concentration of H_3O^+ ions is higher.

$$2H_3O^+(aq) + CaCO_3(s) \rightarrow Ca^{2+}(aq) + CO_2(g) + H_2O(l) \qquad \text{Equation 3}$$

The effect of chloride ion and acetate ion on the pH and reactivity of hydrochloric acid and acetic acid, respectively, further distinguishes the behavior of strong versus weak acids. Adding chloride ion does not change either the pH or activity of the HCl solution. Equation 1 takes place in one direction only—ionization of HCl is essentially irreversible. Adding acetate ion to acetic acid, however, increases the pH from 2 to almost 5 and slows down its rate of reaction with $CaCO_3$. The H_3O^+ concentration in the mixed acetic acid/sodium acetate solution is 100–1000× lower than in acetic acid itself. Equation 2 is thus effectively reversed in the presence of acetate, the "common ion." Ionization of acetic acid is reversible (Equation 4) and the equilibrium constant for this reaction is very small (approx. 10^{-5}).

$$CH_3COOH(aq) + H_2O(l) \rightleftharpoons H_3O^+(aq) + CH_3COO^-(aq) \qquad \text{Equation 4}$$

Demonstrations

Teacher Notes

Buffer Balancing Acts
Chemical Demonstration

Introduction

Buffers provide an essential acid–base balancing act—in consumer products, foods, lakes and streams, even living cells. What are buffers made of and how do they work? This demonstration explores the properties of buffers and their consumer applications.

Concepts

- pH
- Weak acid
- Buffer
- Conjugate base

Materials

Bromthymol blue indicator, 0.1%, 5 mL
Hydrochloric acid, HCl, 1 M, 50 mL*
Sodium hydroxide, NaOH, 1 M, 50 mL*
Sodium phosphate monobasic, NaH_2PO_4, 0.1 M, 200 mL
Sodium phosphate dibasic, Na_2HPO_4, 0.1 M, 200 mL

Alka-Seltzer® tablets, 2
Beakers, 400-mL, 4
Beral-type pipets, 2
Graduated cylinders, 10-mL and 250-mL
Stirring rod
Universal indicator, 5 mL
Water, distilled or deionized

*Dilute to 0.5 M for use in Part A.

Safety Precautions

Hydrochloric acid and sodium hydroxide solutions are corrosive liquids. Avoid exposure to eyes and skin. Universal indicator solution is an alcohol-based solution and is flammable. Avoid exposure to flames and other ignition sources. Wear chemical splash goggles and chemical-resistant gloves and apron. Consult current Material Safety Data Sheets for additional safety, handling, and disposal information.

Procedure

Part A. What Is a Buffer?

1. Mix together 200 mL each of 0.1 M NaH_2PO_4 (sodium phosphate monobasic) and 0.1 M Na_2HPO_4 (sodium phosphate dibasic) to prepare 400 mL of a pH 7 phosphate buffer.

2. Set up four 400-mL beakers and label them #1–4.

3. Add 200 mL of distilled water to beakers #1 and 3.

4. Add 200 mL of the phosphate buffer to beakers #2 and 4.

5. Add about 2 mL of bromthymol blue indicator to each beaker. *(The solutions should all be green. This is the "neutral" color of the indicator, corresponding to pH values of 6–7.6.)*

6. Add 5 drops of 0.5 M HCl to beaker #1. *(Note the color change to yellow. This is the "acidic" color of the indicator.)*

For best results, use either bottled water or freshly distilled water as the control in beakers #1 and 3. Distilled water absorbs large amounts of CO_2 from the air during storage, and may turn yellow with bromthymol blue (Step 5). If this is the case, add a small amount of the buffer to get it to turn green.

87   Buffer Balancing Acts

Demonstrations

Teacher Notes

7. Add 5 drops of 0.5 M HCl to beaker #2. *(No color change—solution stays green).*

8. Add an extra 5 drops of 0.5 M HCl to beaker #2. *(Still no color change. Look frustrated!)*

9. Use a graduated cylinder to add 5 mL of 0.5 M HCl to beaker #2. *(The frustration mounts.)* Continue adding 0.5 M HCl in 5-mL increments until the color changes to yellow. *(This will probably take 2–3 more 5-mL portions of HCl.)*

10. What will happen if strong base is added? Repeat steps 6–9 using beakers #3 and 4 and 0.5 M NaOH instead of HCl. *(Note the color change to blue—the "basic" color of the indicator. The phosphate buffer is an ideal buffer and is thus equally effective in resisting pH changes due to both acid and base.)*

11. Pour the solutions down the drain and rinse the beakers with water for use in Part B.

Part B. Buffer Action in a Consumer Product

1. Set up four clean beakers and relabel them #1–4, if necessary.

2. Add 200 mL of distilled or deionized water to each beaker.

3. Dissolve one Alka-Seltzer® tablet in each beaker #2 and 4.

4. Read the label on the Alka-Seltzer tablet and note the principal ingredients listed. Are there any weak acids and weak bases present that are capable of forming a buffer? *(The active buffer ingredients are citric acid and sodium bicarbonate.)*

5. Add about 20 drops (1 mL) of universal indicator to each beaker #1–4. Note the color and use the color chart to estimate the initial pH of each solution. *(The solutions should all be yellow-green, pH 6–7.)*

6. Add 1 mL of 1 M HCl to beakers #1 and 2. Compare the indicator color and pH of each solution. *(Water will turn red, pH ≤ 4. The Alka-Seltzer solution should stay green, pH 6–7.)*

7. Continue adding 1 M HCl in 1-mL increments to the Alka-Seltzer solution in beaker #2 until the indicator color is the same as that in beaker #1. How much acid must be added to overwhelm the buffer capacity of one Alka-Seltzer tablet? *(This will probably take about 20 mL of 1 M HCl.)*

8. Relate the acid-neutralizing ability of Alka-Seltzer to the definition and uses of antacids.

9. Repeat steps 6 and 7 using beakers #3 and 4 and 1 M NaOH instead of HCl. *(Water immediately turns purple, pH ≥ 10. Alka-Seltzer acts as a buffer against both acid and base.)*

Disposal

Waste solutions may be disposed of down the drain with excess water according to Flinn Scientific Disposal Method #26b. Please consult your current *Flinn Scientific Catalog/Reference Manual* for general guidelines and specific procedures governing the disposal of laboratory waste.

Flinn ChemTopic® Labs — Acids and Bases

Demonstrations

Teacher Notes

Discussion

The ability of buffers to resist changes in pH upon addition of strong acid or base can be traced to their chemical composition. All buffers contain a mixture of both a weak acid (HA) and its conjugate base (A−). The buffer components HA and A− are related to each other by means of the ionization reaction that describes the behavior of a weak acid in water (Equation 1).

$$\underset{\text{weak acid}}{HA} + H_2O \rightleftharpoons \underset{\text{conjugate base}}{A^-} + H_3O^+ \qquad \textit{Equation 1}$$

Buffers control pH because the two buffer components react with and neutralize strong acid or strong base added to the solution. The weak acid component HA reacts with sodium hydroxide to give water and the conjugate base component A− (Equation 2). The conjugate base component A− reacts with hydrochloric acid to give its acid partner HA and chloride ion (Equation 3).

$$HA + NaOH \rightarrow NaA + H_2O \qquad \textit{Equation 2}$$

$$A^- + HCl \rightarrow HA + Cl^- \qquad \textit{Equation 3}$$

Buffer activity will continue as long as both components remain present in solution. If one of the components A− or HA is completely consumed, however, the buffer capacity will be exhausted and the buffer will no longer be effective.

The pH of the phosphate buffer used in Part A is about 7.2, corresponding to the second ionization constant of phosphoric acid (Equations 4 and 5). At equal molar concentrations of HPO_4^{2-} and $H_2PO_4^-$, Equation 5 reduces to $[H_3O^+] = 6.2 \times 10^{-8}$. *Note:* pH = $-\log[H_3O^+]$ = 7.2.

$$H_2PO_4^- + H_2O \rightleftharpoons HPO_4^{2-} + H_3O^+ \qquad \textit{Equation 4}$$

$$K_{a2} = \frac{[HPO_4^{2-}][H_3O^+]}{[H_2PO_4^-]} = 6.2 \times 10^{-8} \qquad \textit{Equation 5}$$

Alka-Seltzer contains 325 mg aspirin, 1.9 g sodium bicarbonate, and 1 g citric acid per tablet. The active "antacid" or buffering ingredients are sodium bicarbonate (0.022 moles), a weak base, and citric acid (0.005 moles), a weak acid. Citric acid is a triprotic acid (three ionizable hydrogens). When the tablet dissolves in water, one mole of citric acid reacts with three moles of bicarbonate ion. The products of the neutralization reaction are citrate ion, carbon dioxide ("plop-plop-fizz-fizz") and water (Equation 6). Citrate ion is the conjugate base of a weak acid and thus acts as a buffer when strong acid is added (Equation 7). Excess sodium bicarbonate, on the other hand, provides buffering action against the addition of strong base (Equation 8).

$$H_3C_6H_5O_7(aq) + 3HCO_3^-(aq) \rightleftharpoons C_6H_5O_7^{3-}(aq) + 3H_2O(l) + 3CO_2(g) \qquad \textit{Equation 6}$$

$$C_6H_5O_7^{3-}(aq) + 3H_3O^+(aq) \rightarrow H_3C_6H_5O_7(aq) + 3H_2O(l) \qquad \textit{Equation 7}$$

$$HCO_3^-(aq) + OH^-(aq) \rightarrow CO_3^{2-}(aq) + H_2O(l) \qquad \textit{Equation 8}$$

Safety and Disposal

Safety and Disposal Guidelines

Safety Guidelines

Teachers owe their students a duty of care to protect them from harm and to take reasonable precautions to prevent accidents from occurring. A teacher's duty of care includes the following:

- Supervising students in the classroom.
- Providing adequate instructions for students to perform the tasks required of them.
- Warning students of the possible dangers involved in performing the activity.
- Providing safe facilities and equipment for the performance of the activity.
- Maintaining laboratory equipment in proper working order.

Safety Contract

The first step in creating a safe laboratory environment is to develop a safety contract that describes the rules of the laboratory for your students. Before a student ever sets foot in a laboratory, the safety contract should be reviewed and then signed by the student and a parent or guardian. Please contact Flinn Scientific at 800-452-1261 or visit the Flinn Website at www.flinnsci.com to request a free copy of the Flinn Scientific Safety Contract.

To fulfill your duty of care, observe the following guidelines:

1. **Be prepared.** Practice all experiments and demonstrations beforehand. Never perform a lab activity if you have not tested it, if you do not understand it, or if you do not have the resources to perform it safely.

2. **Set a good example.** The teacher is the most visible and important role model. Wear your safety goggles whenever you are working in the lab, even (or especially) when class is not in session. Students learn from your good example—whether you are preparing reagents, testing a procedure, or performing a demonstration.

3. **Maintain a safe lab environment.** Provide high-quality goggles that offer adequate protection and are comfortable to wear. Make sure there is proper safety equipment in the laboratory and that it is maintained in good working order. Inspect all safety equipment on a regular basis to ensure its readiness.

4. **Start with safety.** Incorporate safety into each laboratory exercise. Begin each lab period with a discussion of the properties of the chemicals or procedures used in the experiment and any special precautions—including goggle use—that must be observed. Pre-lab assignments are an ideal mechanism to ensure to ensure that students are prepared for lab and understand the safety precautions. Record all safety instruction in your lesson plan.

5. **Proper instruction.** Demonstrate new or unusual laboratory procedures before every activity. Instruct students on the safe way to handle chemicals, glassware, and equipment.

Safety and Disposal

6. **Supervision.** Never leave students unattended—always provide adequate supervision. Work with school administrators to make sure that class size does not exceed the capacity of the room or your ability to maintain a safe lab environment. Be prepared and alert to what students are doing so that you can prevent accidents before they happen.

7. **Understand your resources.** Know yourself, your students, and your resources. Use discretion in choosing experiments and demonstrations that match your background and fit within the knowledge and skill level of your students and the resources of your classroom. You are the best judge of what will work or not. Do not perform any activities that you feel are unsafe, that you are uncomfortable performing, or that you do not have the proper equipment for.

Safety Precautions

Specific safety precautions have been written for every experiment and demonstration in this book. The safety information describes the hazardous nature of each chemical and the specific precautions that must be followed to avoid exposure or accidents. The safety section also alerts you to potential dangers in the procedure or techniques. Regardless of what lab program you use, it is important to maintain a library of current Material Safety Data Sheets for all chemicals in your inventory. Please consult current MSDS for additional safety, handling, and disposal information.

Disposal Procedures

The disposal procedures included in this book are based on the Suggested Laboratory Chemical Disposal Procedures found in the *Flinn Scientific Catalog/Reference Manual*. The disposal procedures are only suggestions—do not use these procedures without first consulting with your local government regulatory officials.

Many of the experiments and demonstrations produce small volumes of aqueous solutions that can be flushed down the drain with excess water. Do not use this procedure if your drains empty into groundwater through a septic system or into a storm sewer. Local regulations may be more strict on drain disposal than the practices suggested in this book and in the *Flinn Scientific Catalog/Reference Manual*. You must determine what types of disposal procedures are permitted in your area—contact your local authorities.

Any suggested disposal method that includes "discard in the trash" requires your active attention and involvement. Make sure that the material is no longer reactive, is placed in a suitable container (plastic bag or bottle), and is in accordance with local landfill regulations. Please do not inadvertently perform any extra "demonstrations" due to unpredictable chemical reactions occurring in your trash can. Think before you throw!

Finally, please read all the narratives before you attempt any Suggested Laboratory Chemical Disposal Procedure found in your current *Flinn Scientific Catalog/Reference Manual*.

Flinn Scientific is your most trusted and reliable source of reference, safety, and disposal information for all chemicals used in the high school science lab. To request a complementary copy of the most recent *Flinn Scientific Catalog/Reference Manual,* call us at 800-452-1261 or visit our website at www.flinnsci.com.

National Science Education Standards

Experiments and Demonstrations

Content Standards	Properties of Acids and Bases	Natural Indicators	Measuring Acid Strength	Classic Titration	Microscale Titration	Buffers Keep the Balance	Indicator Sponge	The Rainbow Tube	Upset Tummy? MOM to the Rescue!	Strong vs. Weak Acids	Buffer Balancing Acts
Unifying Concepts and Processes											
Systems, order, and organization	✓					✓					✓
Evidence, models, and explanation	✓	✓	✓			✓	✓		✓	✓	✓
Constancy, change, and measurement	✓	✓	✓	✓	✓	✓	✓		✓	✓	✓
Evolution and equilibrium			✓			✓			✓		✓
Form and function											
Science as Inquiry											
Identify questions and concepts that guide scientific investigation	✓	✓	✓	✓	✓	✓	✓		✓	✓	✓
Design and conduct scientific investigations	✓	✓	✓	✓	✓	✓				✓	✓
Use technology and mathematics to improve scientific investigations			✓	✓	✓						
Formulate and revise scientific explanations and models using logic and evidence	✓	✓	✓	✓	✓	✓	✓		✓	✓	✓
Recognize and analyze alternative explanations and models	✓		✓			✓			✓	✓	✓
Communicate and defend a scientific argument											
Understanding scientific inquiry	✓	✓	✓				✓		✓		
Physical Science											
Structure of atoms											
Structure and properties of matter	✓	✓	✓			✓			✓	✓	✓
Chemical reactions	✓	✓	✓	✓	✓	✓	✓	✓	✓	✓	✓
Motions and forces											
Conservation of energy and the increase in disorder											
Interactions of energy and matter											

National Science Education Standards

Experiments and Demonstrations

Content Standards (continued)	Properties of Acids and Bases	Natural Indicators	Measuring Acid Strength	Classic Titration	Microscale Titration	Buffers Keep the Balance	Indicator Sponge	The Rainbow Tube	Upset Tummy? MOM to the Rescue!	Strong vs. Weak Acids	Buffer Balancing Acts
Science and Technology											
Identify a problem or design an opportunity				✓							
Propose designs and choose between alternative solutions											
Implement a proposed solution											
Evaluate the solution and its consequences											
Communicate the problem, process, and solution											
Understand science and technology				✓							
Science in Personal and Social Perspectives											
Personal and community health						✓					✓
Population growth											
Natural resources						✓					✓
Environmental quality						✓					✓
Natural and human-induced hazards						✓					✓
Science and technology in local, national, and global challenges											
History and Nature of Science											
Science as a human endeavor		✓									
Nature of scientific knowledge	✓	✓	✓	✓	✓	✓	✓		✓	✓	✓
Historical perspectives	✓	✓									

Master Materials Guide

(for a class of 30 students working in pairs)

Experiments and Demonstrations

Chemicals	Flinn Scientific Catalog No.	Properties of Acids and Bases	Natural Indicators	Measuring Acid Strength	Classic Titration	Microscale Titration	Buffers Keep the Balance	Indicator Sponge	The Rainbow Tube	Upset Tummy? MOM to the Rescue!	Strong vs. Weak Acids	Buffer Balancing Acts
Acetic acid, 0.1 M	A0096	100 mL	100 mL									
Acetic acid, 1 M	A0095										400 mL	
Alka-Seltzer tablets	A0111											2
Ammonium hydroxide solution, 0.1 M	A0098	75 ml	100 mL									
Ammonium nitrate solution, 0.1 M*	A0290		100 mL									
Bromthymol blue indicator solution, 0.04%	B0047		100 mL				75 mL					5 mL
Buffer capsules, pH 2–12 set	B0227		1 set									
Buffer solution, pH 4	B0089			100 mL								
Buffer solution, pH 7	B0092			100 mL								
Calcium carbonate	C0347										40 g	
Congo red indicator	C0120							1 g				
Hydrochloric acid, 0.1 M	H0014	100 mL			600 mL		150 mL	25 mL				
Hydrochloric acid, 1 M	H0013						100 mL				400 mL	50 mL
Hydrochloric acid, 3 M	H0034										20 mL	
Isopropyl ("rubbing,) alcohol, 70%	I0021		750 mL									
Magnesium hydroxide solution, saturated (Milk of Magnesia)	M0122									20 mL		
Magnesium ribbon or turnings	M0139 or M0112	6 g										
Methyl orange indicator solution, 0.1%	M0078		100 mL									
Phenolphthalein indicator solution, 0.5%	P0115	50 mL			25 mL	25 mL	25 mL[†]					
Phosphoric acid, 14.8 M	P0201		10 mL[§]									
Potassium bisulfate (potassium hydrogen sulfate)	P0134				3 g							
Potassium bitartrate (potassium hydrogen tartrate)	P0135				3 g							
Potassium hydrogen phthalate	P0056				3 g							
Potassium phosphate monobasic (potassium dihydrogen phosphate)	P0141				3 g							
Rainbow acid universal indicator	U0012										5 mL	
Sodium acetate	S0344										16 g	
Sodium bicarbonate solution, 0.1 M*	S0385		100 mL				150 mL					
Sodium carbonate solution, saturated	S0233								6 mL			

*Gramolpak is a unique product for the preparation of 1 L of solution of known molarity.
[†]Dilute to 0.05% for microscale applications.
[§]Dilute to 0.1 M

Flinn ChemTopic® Labs — Acids and Bases

Master Materials Guide

(for a class of 30 students working in pairs) — **Experiments and Demonstrations**

	Flinn Scientific Catalog No.	Properties of Acids and Bases	Natural Indicators	Measuring Acid Strength	Classic Titration	Microscale Titration	Buffers Keep the Balance	Indicator Sponge	The Rainbow Tube	Upset Tummy? MOM to the Rescue!	Strong vs. Weak Acids	Buffer Balancing Acts
Chemicals, continued												
Sodium chloride	S0063										12 g	
Sodium hydroxide pellets	S0074				5 g	10 g						
Sodium hydroxide solution, 0.1 M	S0149	150 mL		300 mL	1 L		150 mL					
Sodium hydroxide solution, 1 M	S0148							100 mL				50 mL
Sodium phosphate dibasic solution, 0.1 M*	S0398						250 mL					200 mL
Sodium phosphate monobasic solution, 0.1 M	S0371		100 mL				350 mL					200 mL
Thymol blue indicator solution, 0.04%	T0045		100 mL									
Universal indicator solution	U0002	25 mL					100 mL	3 mL	5 mL			5 mL
Vinegar	V0001					150 mL						
Zinc nitrate solution, 0.1 M	Z0026		100 mL									
Glassware												
Beakers												
50-mL	GP1005					30	30					
100-mL	GP1010		15									
150-mL	GP1015		15	15								
250-mL	GP1020				30							
400-mL	GP1025											4
1-L	GP1040								2	1		
Buret, 50-mL	GP1090				15							
Erlenmeyer flasks												
125-mL	GP3040				15	15						
250-mL	GP3045											
Graduated cylinders												
10-mL	GP2005						30					1
25-mL	GP2010					15				1	1	
100-mL	GP2020				15							
250-mL	GP2025										1	1
Hydrometer cylinder, 600 mL	AP8599										4	
Pipet, volumetric, 10-mL	GP7030				15							
Test tubes												
16 × 150 mm	GP6066						90	1				
Stirring rods	GP5075	15		15			15					1

Continued on next page

Master Materials Guide

(for a class of 30 students working in pairs)

Experiments and Demonstrations

General Equipment and Miscellaneous	Flinn Scientific Catalog No.	Properties of Acids and Bases	Natural Indicators	Measuring Acid Strength	Classic Titration	Microscale Titration	Buffers Keep the Balance	Indicator Sponge	The Rainbow Tube	Upset Tummy? MOM to the Rescue!	Strong vs. Weak Acids	Buffer Balancing Acts
Balance, centigram (0.01-g precision)	OB2059		3	3		3	1				1	
Cellulose sponge	AP1343							1				
Color pencils, assorted	FB0643		15									
Conductivity meter	AP1493	5										
Demonstration tray, large	AP5429										1	
Filter paper	AP3104		15									
Food coloring	V0003							2 mL				
Forceps	AP8328	15										
Funnel	AP3200		15									
Gloves, nitrile, acid-resistant	AP3258							1				
Hot plate	AP4674		optional									
Laboratory Techniques Guide, pkg. of 30*	AP6248		1	1								
LabPro Interface system	TC1500					15						
Litmus paper, neutral	AP7934	1 vial										
LoggerPro Software	TC1421					15						
Magnetic stirrer (optional)	AP6067					15				1		
Mortar and pestle	AP6066		15									
pH meters	AP8673			15								
pH sensor	TC1503					15						
pH Test paper, narrow-range, 6.0–8.0	AP335						1 roll					
pH Test strips, 1–12	AP1107	1 vial										
Pipet filler	AP1887					15						
Pipets, Beral-type, graduated	AP1721	75	75	30			105		2	2		2
Pipets, Beral-type, micro-tip	AP1719					45						
Reaction plate, microscale, 24-well	AP1447	15	15			15	15					
Stirring bars (optional)	AP1090					15				1		
Test tube rack	AP1319						15	1				
Tongs	AP8266							1				
Universal indicator overhead color chart	AP5367							1				
Wash bottle	AP1668	15	15	15	15	15						
Water, distilled or deionized	W0007, W0001	✓	✓	✓	✓	✓	✓			✓	✓	✓
Weighing dishes	AP1278			30								6

*The Laboratory Techniques Guide provides convenient illustrations and explanations of filtration, titration, and 16 other common lab techniques.